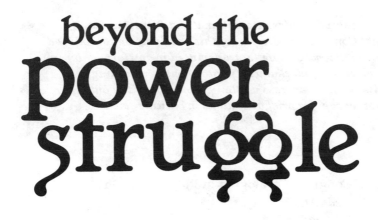

# beyond the
# power
# struggle

susan m. campbell, ph.d.

***Impact*** 🐚 ***Publishers***
SAN LUIS OBISPO, CALIFORNIA 93406

Library of Congress Cataloging in Publication Data
*Campbell, Susan M., 1941-*
   *Beyond the power struggle.*

   *1. Interpersonal relations.     2. Interpersonal conflict —*
*Prevention.     3. Reconciliation.     4. Power (Social sciences)*
*I. Title.*
*HM132.C34     1984          158'.2          84-11846*
*ISBN 0-915166-46-1*

Fifth Printing, January, 1992

Design and cover by Tess Taylor, San Luis Obispo, California.

Printed in the United States of America.

Published by **Impact 🐚 Publishers**
POST OFFICE BOX 1094
SAN LUIS OBISPO, CALIFORNIA 93406

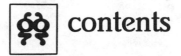 contents

preface

## PUBLISHER'S NOTE

Cabrillo Child Center

Julie Edwards
Cabrillo College
main 479 6352
~ 479 6100

Jamie Kaiser

479 6352
dance

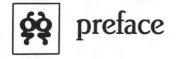 preface

In the workshops and lectures I have conducted across the country since writing *The Couple's Journey*, there is one issue that people raise more than any other: "Does relationship inevitably involve struggle? Aren't there ways to avoid the power struggles that most people encounter, or at least get through them without unnecessary pain?" In the area of human relationships, these questions seem to be on the tip of more people's tongues than all other questions combined.

As a consultant to business organizations in the areas of team building, conflict management and strategic planning, I have encountered a similar recurring theme: how can co-workers with very different ways of doing a job collaborate effectively? How can we learn to be comfortable with one another instead of trying to change one another?

Whether we are dealing with love relationships or those among co-workers, the issue of power struggles and the differences that give rise to them seem to trouble most people at some time in their lives.

Power struggles occur because people are different and because people often like to do things in their own ways. Yet psychological research and common sense tell us that people feel happiest, most vibrant and alive, when they are in agreement or harmony with others, when there is an absence of conflict or struggle. Seen in this light, the question takes on an additional dimension: "Why do we struggle when it feels so good to agree? Why do we go to war, when in our hearts we long for peace?"

Some would argue that conflict is inevitable and that if people knew the answers to these questions, they would still behave as they do now. My observations tell me that differences in perspective are indeed inevitable, but that enduring, unproductive struggles are not. I believe that if people could experience in their everyday lives — with their spouses, with their children, with their bosses — reliable and satisfying ways of resolving differences, there might still be the possibility of peace on this earth.

Susan Campbell
Mill Valley, California
March 1984

# one: From Either-Or to Both-And Relationships

The back door slammed a little harder than usual. In spite of her better judgement, Margie called out, "Daniel, did you wipe your feet?" After 13 years of marriage she knows how to read Daniel's door-slamming signals. She knows he is irritated about something. But she has needs too, and one of them is to keep her freshly-polished kitchen floor clean for tomorrow's dinner guests.

"How was your day?" she inquires as Daniel shuffles mechanically into the living room, unloading books and papers as he goes along.

"Huh?"

"You don't seem to be in a very good mood," she tries again.

"Look, don't tell me what kind of mood I'm in — I feel fine! And how many times do I have to tell you, I'm not one of the children — I *don't* need to be told when to wipe my feet!"

We're at it again, Margie thinks to herself. I just want to express myself, and I wind up putting him off. He never wants to hear about the things that concern *me*.

We're at it again, Daniel thinks to himself. She knows I've had a hard day and she can't wait to start badgering me.

1

Margie and Daniel *are* at it again. This is just a little incident, but it is typical of so many little incidents. They have learned to live with a certain level of tension in their relationship, but each wishes secretly that there were a way to get back the good feelings they once had together.

Have you ever tried and tried to get another person to understand your needs, and found that the harder you tried, the less understanding the other person became? Or that the more you asserted your interests, the more assertive the other became in response?

Many relationships reach a point where the partners have forgotten why they got together in the first place. This can happen at home, at work, in friendships. You may be slighted in some small way, so you return the slight. We do have the power to hurt one another, so to protect ourselves from being hurt, or to respond to a real or imagined hurt, we begin to *disconnect*, to pull the plug on our emotional connection.

Daniel and Margie reacted as most of us do when others seem unsympathetic to our needs: they escalated the situation, asserting their needs even more forcefully. As they felt increasingly disconnected from one another, they became more and more adversarial. They were creating a power struggle...

## Either-Or Thinking and the Power Struggle

"Seek no contract, and you will find union." This ancient Taoist maxim illustrates one of the great paradoxes of human relationships: the harder you try for agreement, accord, communion, the more these qualities elude you. When you are *trying* to be in harmony with others, your attitude belies the fact that you are not. If instead your actions are based on a feeling of connectedness with others, the question of agreement or disagreement becomes irrelevant.

Us and them. Yours and mine. Winners and losers. Some people go through life assuming that their interests are at odds with those of others. They spend a lot of time protecting their own interests. Those who see their interests as aligned with others' feel no such need for protection.

The desire for contracts or other legalistic agreements stems from fear or lack of trust. That same fear and lack of trust leads to *power struggles*: ''Let's write it down so we know who is in control here!'' Such insecurity is not resolved by avoiding contracts or suppressing fears, however. Those approaches simply treat the symptoms and not the cause of the dis-ease. The answer lies in changing one's way of thinking about relationships with other people.

The fears that lead to power struggles are usually based on *either-or thinking*. It is either-or thinking which causes a mother to feel threatened if her son shows special affection for the mother of a friend — because ''if he gives affection to her, he's taking affection from me.'' It implies a closed system, where the other mother's gain is her loss, since ''there's only just so much love to go around.'' People believe that *either* you get your way *or* I get mine, and the world they create reflects this attitude.

If we are to have any chance at all of experiencing the world's abundance, we first need to change our thinking about the kind of world we live in. We need to change our habitual way of constructing what we think of as real. Most of us have been conditioned to think in either-or terms, to divide our world up into bits and pieces and parts, each segment having a separate and independent existence of its own. In childhood, we had your toys and my toys. In adolescence, we had the in-group and the out-group. In adulthood, we have success and failure.

In relationships, according to the either-or mind set, we have your needs and my needs, your way of doing or seeing things and mine. And when you assert yours, I feel threatened and protective of mine.

Do you tend to feel more comfortable with others when they agree with you and less so when they disagree with you? It's a common reaction, and it suggests a feeling of threat associated with differences or disagreement. Many people are unaware that they feel threatened by differences. They simply know they feel uncomfortable around certain people. But why should anyone feel threatened or uncomfortable when confronted with a difference in viewpoint? Because most of us were taught that *either* your way *or* my way is valid. We rarely consider the possibility that *both* may be!

The way out of the either-or trap, the way to get beyond the struggle-oriented mind set, is to begin to think in *both-and* terms. This expansion allows in more information. It is like like changing a camera's lens from standard to wide angle. You can see more all at once, and this allows you to see interconnectedness among things you once thought to be separate.

## The Expanded View: Both-And in Action

I once owned a house in a "nicer" section of an old New England town. It was the custom in that neighborhood to keep the Cape Cod style homes neatly painted, the shrubbery well-groomed and the lawns freshly mowed. After I had been living there for about six months, I noticed that my next door neighbor, Shady Houlihan, had begun to neglect the upkeep of his property. The paint on his house had begun to peel noticeably. He had stopped mowing his lawn. And he was often seen sitting in his front yard in a rusty old lawn chair, unshaven, nursing a bottle of whiskey. My first impulse — and that of several other neighbors — was to somehow make him feel unwelcome in the neighborhood, in hopes that he would decide to move. We feared that the condition of his place would affect our property values.

During one neighborhood gathering, several of us were bemoaning the continued deterioration of Shady's place when someone mentioned that it had all started when he lost his job as a postman. He'd held the job for 15 years, had been unable to find another and had become depressed. As the discussion continued, someone else suggested that if anyone could help Shady find work, he might recover. We might all be spared continued concern over declining property values and deteriorating appearance of the neighborhood.

I remembered a Federal grant that had recently funded a teen drop-in center in a nearby town. One of the positions that had not yet been filled was that of caretaker. I decided to talk to Shady to let him know about this possibility of work. Shady showed considerable interest and aptitude for the position and eventually took the job. His depression lifted. He began to take care of his house and yard. And everyone in the neighborhood felt good about having a hand in Shady's recovery.

Like most stories, this one has a moral. When Shady's neighbors were seeing the world in *separative* terms, with us on the right side of the fence and him on the wrong side, all we could think of was how to get rid of Shady. This was a highly unrealistic solution because his was the only house in the neighborhood which was not owned mostly by the bank. His home was paid for. He'd lived in the neighborhood longer than any of us, and it was almost certain that he was there to stay. Thus, not only was the separative solution self-centered, it was also impractical. When our thinking shifted toward a view which emphasized our *connectedness* to Shady, as neighbors with a common interest and as fellow humans, then we were able to achieve a solution that was both practical and humane.

Seeing the world with an expanded view that shows how interconnected we are with our neighbors can help us bring new resources to bear on problems, resources we might never otherwise discover.

Seeing the world in separate parts, and yourself as separate from your fellow humans, can justify behaving in terms of narrow self-interest. When we step back to see the larger picture, we may find that it is ourselves we have hurt.

In close love and work relationships, the awareness of our interdependence usually comes naturally. The needs and views of *both* people seek harmonious expression — or at least peaceful coexistence. Without this, the relationship feels incomplete.

Yet most of us resist the experience of a deep and abiding harmony, even as we long for it. There seems to be a fear of what we may lose in merging with another, which can overshadow our hope of what we may gain. This simultaneous wish for harmony, alongside the fear of losing our individuality, leads to inner conflict. We seem unable to allow fear and hope to gracefully coexist within our psyches.

If we could break the habit of either-or thinking, which conditions us to pursue either harmony or individuality, we could see the larger picture — and perhaps recognize that both needs naturally occur together and can be satisfied together.

## Reconciling the Irreconcilable

After spending the first 35 years of my life in a state of almost perpetual ambivalence, I began to search for relief. I was beginning to get awfully tired of the amount of energy I was wasting on this pattern of recurring inner conflict. Sometimes I seemed to feel peaceful and contented with my life, but I now believe that this was because the conflict had temporarily receded into the background of my awareness — I was simply busy with other things.

Do I express my anger or my hurt? Do I feel happy or sad? Do I love him or hate him? I was constantly plagued by questions such as these. I couldn't seem to settle on one way or the other to feel or to act.

Then one day I had an unexpected insight into another state of consciousness. I was co-leading a week-long encounter group at a Quaker retreat center in upstate New York. The theme of the workshop was ''Encounter and Silence.'' By about the fifth day of the group, almost all of the 28 participants had experienced a significant catharsis or illumination. As the leader, I had not allowed myself the luxury of a deep emotional experience, however. I had been maintaining an air of composure and control as people all around me were having breakdowns and breakthroughs.

I began to notice that, although I could feel empathy with others' feelings, my own emotional sensitivity was becoming more and more blunted as the week wore on. It seemed as if I might be trying to armor myself against the intrusion of my own pain, so that I could pay attention to that of the others. Yet their pain was subtly stimulating similar feelings within me. I tried to pretend everything was all right with me. I played my role as group leader competently and effectively.

On the evening of the fifth day, the dam broke. Holding myself back from the group had led me to a stark awareness of my aloneness. I wept openly and told the group of my almost constant struggle with my inner ambivalence — a struggle which I had hidden from others since it first developed in my late adolescence. I seemed always to be of two minds, sometimes more. Everyone around me had always seemed so definite, so certain. I, on the other hand, could never decide what I felt because I always felt such a mixture of things. As I babbled and wept and allowed myself to be comforted, I slowly began to feel a strange and different sensation welling up within me, a feeling of utter despair entwined with a feeling of profound joy. It was a sensation that could not be called either despair or joy. I was neither happy nor sad, nor was I ambivalent. I was happy-sad: both grateful and despairing for my state as a human being, both trusting and insecure, both confident and helpless.

This experience is almost as vivid in my mind today as it was on that night, almost ten years ago. I will always remember the sense of wholeness, the freedom from inner conflict that I felt. My ambivalence had become two-sidedness rather than oppositeness, polarity rather than polarization. I experienced myself as *both-and* instead of *either-or*.

Somehow, and I can't say exactly how, my way of seeing things changed after that. I didn't demand of myself a choice between feelings like love and anger, fear and hope, joy and sadness. I let whatever was inside me be there, without trying to straighten things out or hide the messiness of my internal state. I still experienced mixed emotions, perhaps even more so than before. But they didn't feel so troublesome. I stopped trying to make myself "normal." And in the process I stopped feeling "crazy."

As time has passed and my lifework has come to focus on interpersonal relationships, I am beginning to see that many of the struggles that bring people pain in their relationships are similar to my struggle within myself. When you try to sort things out into neat little boxes, putting love over here and anger over there, fear in this box and trust in that one, you violate something about the *natural messiness* of things. When you expect B to follow A because it did once before, when you expect intentions to lead you in the intended direction, you ignore the absolute interconnectedness of everything alive.

I believe that this interconnectedness, mixed-upness or both-and-ness underlies the experience of what most people might call paradox or irony. You know the feeling: the harder you try to make something happen, the less likely it seems to occur. Or the more fully you come to know something, the more mysterious it seems. Or the more you come to love someone, the more they seem to provoke your anger. If experiences such as these cause you pain or puzzlement, perhaps it's time to learn more about both-and thinking. Many of our experiences don't seem to make sense when we think of them in the ordinary ways that we were taught. Our lives are full of paradoxes, or so it seems. But there is a more expanded, wide-angle view available to us. It is possible to relax and enjoy life's ironies!

In the chapters which follow, we'll take a look at how our difficulty accepting the both-and view leads us into a life of struggle. And we'll discover some new ways to open ourselves to a broader perspective, to gain a vision of what lies beyond the power struggle.

# two: Power Struggle and Paradox

I'd like to share with you some of the relationship paradoxes which I have encountered, and from which I have learned that life is to be experienced, not solved.

## The Paradox of Surrender

Not long ago I began to notice that the harder I tried to achieve a particular type of relationship or to create a particular impression, the more these goals eluded me. Much to my surprise, when I *let go* of my attachment to how I wanted things to be, what I had been seeking did come to me!

• The more I tried to get my husband to *want* to make love with me, the more turned off he seemed to get. But when I accepted and appreciated the attentions he did give me, instead of concentrating on what *I* wanted, he ''magically'' became more loving.

• The more conscientiously I tried to ignore my husband's comments about former lovers (in the hope that he would soon stop doing this), the more he indulged his fantasies of the past. When I told him I was bothered by it, at the risk of making a big deal out of a minor irritation, he stopped. My ''ignoring'' it was actually making it into a bigger deal than mentioning it to him. When I let it go, he felt

my relaxation and allowed himself to be influenced by my
wishes — in a way that he could not when he felt my
ill-concealed tension.

   •   When I tried to get my employees to work in the
logical and organized way that I did, things in the office would
get more and more chaotic and disorganized. When I came to
know and trust each person's unique work style, after much
discussion on the subject, I relaxed my concern with their
sloppiness, and their work suddenly became more orderly.

   Why do things often happen this way? Were people out
to thwart my desires or teach me a lesson? Or was there
another principle at work here? I believe the answer has to do
with what I call "the paradox of surrender." When I am
terribly attached to having something happen a certain way,
that is usually when I will be frustrated. When I am relaxed
about the outcome, I am more apt to be satisfied.

   Attachment to having what I want seems to almost
always be accompanied by a fear that I won't get it. This fear
tends to inhibit the free exchange of energy between myself
and another. We become less open to one another, less able to
feel our natural empathy and connectedness with one
another, less able to anticipate each others' needs. Thus,
things often become discordant for no apparent reason. My
lovers and co-workers were probably not intentionally
resisting me. They just couldn't feel a clear, trustworthy
connection to me anymore.

   I have a friend, Harvey Bergdorf, whose situation clearly
illustrates the paradox of surrender. Harvey is always saying
to me, "I want so much to find a deep lasting love relationship
that I seem to scare women away." This statement shows that
Harvey already has a clue about why his lovers always leave
him. It also contains a plea for deeper understanding of his
situation.

   As I think about my friend now, recalling the stories he
has told me of the ups and downs of his love life, I'd like to
speculate about what may be at the root of Harvey's
unluckiness in love. Embedded in his wish for love is an even

stronger *fear* that he won't find it. On top of this, he is angry
at women in general because he has been hurt so often. And,
as if that weren't enough to scare women away, he also feels a
bit sorry for himself. Whenever he pursues the attentions of
an atttractive woman, he carries this negative emotional
"baggage" with him. The woman can intuit the extra load
Harvey is carrying, and although she may be attracted to him,
she can't seem to get close to him. She herself may not even
understand her negative response. It doesn't make rational
sense. Harvey is an attractive guy. But there is something
about the psychological space between the two would-be
lovers that is cluttered. Harvey's baggage is in the way. He
holds his fears and negative expectations so closely to him
that there is no room for a woman's love.

Viewing the situation superficially, you'd think an
attractive, eligible bachelor like Harvey could have his pick of
women. But when we look at those relationships in more
detail, we see not just Harvey but the emotional climate
between him and the women in his life. Only then do we see
his fears — and her reactions to his fears — as important
ingredients in the relationship.

If Harvey or his women friends could sense this
interference with their mutual openness, they might then see
themselves holding so tightly to how they want it to be, or how
they fear it will be, that they cannot feel how it is. Usually
conscious recognition and acceptance of a condition are
necessary before change can occur. Harvey needs to admit
how tightly he is holding on to his fears before he can begin to
let them go.

## My Search For Mr. Right

For a long time in my life I had a complete image of the
type of man I wanted for a mate. He would be adventuresome,
athletic, oriented toward personal and spiritual development,
but above all, confidently settled in his life's vocation. I
wanted him to have achieved his vocational goals so that he
would not be constantly striving to prove himself. I had been

frustrated too often in relationships with men who were so busy proving themselves in their careers that they had no time or energy left for a relationship. During this period of my search for Mr. Right, with this picture clearly in mind, I found myself coldly and methodically rejecting many potential suitors.

Then, inexplicably, I fell in love with a man who not only didn't have his career settled, he didn't even have aspirations *toward* a career! Now, this was a new one for me, a situation for which I was totally unprepared. It fit nowhere in my well-laid plans. And I must admit I fought it for quite some time. I couldn't picture myself with this type of man. In my mind I'd grown attached to a fantasied Mr. Right whom I'd never met, while here and now in my flesh and blood life was a man whom I loved but could not let myself enjoy. I suffered for almost a year with this dilemma before I opened myself to embrace what I had instead of continuing to be hung up on what I didn't have. When I opened up, I saw something quite startling. I had wanted a man who had his career settled so he'd have time for me. Well, this man didn't have a career, but he certainly did have time. I'd been unable to appreciate this fact as long as I was attached to having things just so. When I let go of my picture of Mr. Right, I was able to see that the man I had was more right for me than I could have imagined!

Surrendering or letting go of attachments does not mean forgetting about your wants or needs. It means relaxing your mind enough so that you stop straining to get what you want. Often when you stop worrying about what you don't have, your attention becomes more open and available to perceiving and appreciating what you do have. This tends to lead to the experience of enjoyment. Once in this state of enjoyment, you become more attractive, thus increasing your chances for getting what you want. I'm reminded of the old saying, ''The rich get richer and the poor get poorer.'' But in this case, we are talking about those who are rich in the spirit of joy and contentment. When you are in such a state, you tend to attract others who are in a similar state. You also tend to bring out the best in those around you, thus further surrounding yourself with riches.

## The Paradox of Avoidance

Related to the paradox of surrender is another familiar one: the more I try to avoid a situation, the more it seems to recur in my life. Reflecting back on the significant love relationships in my life, there has been, until recently, one recurring pattern. For many years I was always the main breadwinner in the family. Every time I ended a relationship, I would vow not to get involved again with someone whom I'd have to fully or partly support. But pretty soon, I'd be in love again, and I would forget my vow. I had plenty of opportunities to become involved with men who could support me, but ironically, I could never become interested in these men. It seemed I was running away from the other situation so fast that I kept bumping into it.

What was going on here? Once again we encounter our old familiar culprit, fear. I radiated my fears like a neon sign, fears that I would never be supported, fears that I would never know the feeling of being taken care of, even in some small way. While I thought I was choosing my partners consciously, my fears had generated an unconscious self-fulfilling prophecy. I'd given so much energy to the situation by trying to avoid it, that I attracted it time and again.

Now that this pattern seems to have resolved itself, I can look at my situation with more perspective. I think the pattern stopped pursuing me when I stopped running, when I began to let myself enjoy supporting the man I was with. I realized that I was doing exactly what I wanted to be doing with my life and with my time. I love to work and earning money happens to come easily. Why shouldn't I share what I have, I asked myself. As I stopped worrying about whether I was being supported and stopped protesting the lack of support I was experiencing, support came to me. In my case it did not come in the form of a rich partner. My financial support came from the sale of some real estate I'd owned for quite some time. I'd planned to get a large sum of money so I could buy a house, but instead, because of the buyer's financing problems, I was given a note guaranteeing me a monthly income for the rest of my life.

This example shows the similarity between the paradox of avoidance and the paradox of surrender. The one is in a sense the converse of the other. To stop avoiding or resisting is to surrender. The difference is that when you surrender, you stop trying to force a change in your circumstances, whereas when you stop avoiding, you stop running away from your circumstances.

There's an old saying, "You can run, but you can't hide." This saying summarizes the principle behind the paradox of avoidance. If there is a feature in your character that repeatedly causes you pain or frustration, this feature will haunt you until the day you die, unless you face it squarely and deal with it.

I became painfully aware of this principle as I watched my own grandparents become aged and then senile. During their middle age, they could run away from their fears and paranoia through overwork. But as the body weakened and the capacity for work slackened, so did their rigid avoidance system. My grandfather's fear that people would take advantage of him began to haunt him like a recurring nightmare. And the fact that he was old and vulnerable did in fact make him an easy and tempting mark for con artists, selling everything from caskets to lifetime-guaranteed roofing. Grandpa had always seemed a bit paranoid to me, but only in later life did his fears take over his personality. He had spent his entire life avoiding being ripped off, only to have his worst fears come true at the end of his life.

In offering these illustrations of how you can't run away from yourself, I am not saying that you cannot intentionally eschew your less constructive habits or qualities. If you can face and acknowledge these qualities in yourself, then you are in a good position to consciously give them less and less time on the stage of your personal drama. This is not avoiding them. This is taking responsibility for them so that they will be less likely to show up in untoward ways and places.

## The Paradox of Understanding

A third relationship paradox involves the experience of knowing another person deeply. Often the more intimately I have come to know another, the more I can love and appreciate him, and in a sense, the more connected I feel to him. Yet at the same time, the more I know about another, the more I see our differences and areas of potential misunderstanding. The more I know him, the more reasons I find for loving him and at the same time the more reasons I see for leaving him. As I see him in greater depth and in a wider variety of situations, I see the ways in which he is absolutely himself, not an extension of me. This brings me to let go of needing him to be a certain way in conformity to my needs.

As this process of letting go is occurring, it has often felt at first as if I am becoming detached, indifferent or less loving toward my partner. This is not really the case, unless I am harboring anger about the realization that he is beyond my control. Ordinarily, the true appreciation of other-ness is accompanied by a calming and cooling down of the fire in the relationship, for much of the fire has to do with projections and fantasies.

Along with this cooling and calming comes a fullness, a sense of being satisfied with how it is, a letting go of the images and expectations of how it should be. I call this the paradox of understanding. The more I come to know another, the more I see the impossibility of completely understanding him. And as I accept this fact, my alienation dissolves into a deeper sense of understanding. I come to a point in the relationship where I realize that our differences, like our similarities, don't really make any difference when it comes to loving one another.

Realizations such as this can only come when I am able to remember to observe my reality through the wide-angle lens of past-present-future, as one continuity in time. The way I feel today may be altered radically by the day after tomorrow. The only way to get a consistent picture is to view things from the widest possible angle.

In the research I conducted for *The Couple's Journey,* I found that most couples need to experience ups and downs together before reaching the Stability Stage. After several years of loving and sharing and struggling, people begin to realize the source of their ups and downs. They see that sometimes their differences and disagreements cause pain and sometimes they do not. They become aware that it is not differences but one's *resistance* to differences that causes pain. And while it is true that the longer two people live or work together, the more differences they encounter, time can also bring a broadened perspective on these differences, and a lessening of the resistance to them.

Viewing your relationship from a broad time perspective allows you to see your differences in their context: a stable mosaic of experiences, somewhat changing, somewhat constant. Such a perspective is basic to the feeling of understanding.

## The Iatrogenic Paradox

Medical researchers have found that new illnesses tend to occur in the population just as cures for these illnesses become available to medical science. Also, as the cure becomes more readily available, the incidence of an illness will increase. The more advanced the techology became for detecting and treating skin cancer, for example, the more cases of this disease were reported. As more people became trained as marriage counselors, more couples experienced problems in getting along.

In my own close loving and working relationships, I have observed that the better we become at resolving our interpersonal differences, the more differences we encounter.

The more skilled we become at solving problems, the more problems we have. This seemed to me unfair at times. But as I became better able to solve problems, problems were no longer a nuisance. They were simply events calling for attention. Thus, once again as my perspective expanded, as I was able to feel both my problem-solving capacities and my limitations needing corrective action, the apparent contradiction dissolved.

It is said that life never confronts you with any problem that is too big for you to handle. This statement may be simply a way of giving comfort to people in adversity. On the other hand, it reminds me that often it is the people who know best how to solve problems or face challenges that we find taking on even bigger challenges.

In ashrams or other centers for spiritual development, teachers always give the harder tasks to the more advanced pupils. This is true in most educational systems. Thus, if you pursue self-development because you think it will make your life easier, you may be surprised. Yet your surprise may not be altogether unpleasant, since you may find as you develop yourself that you no longer desire a problem-free life. You may even find yourself seeking out challenges that stretch your talents and capacities.

## The Paradox of Responsibility

People who have been working for a while to develop their self-understanding realize that each of us is responsible for her or his own mental state or mood. Yet at the same time we see how affected we are by the moods of others close to us. Conversely, we know that the quality of our feelings and thoughts can profoundly affect those around us. You are responsible for the quality of your own state of mind, and at the same time you are responsible for the ''waves'' you create around you, which influence others.

When I am feeling anxiety, I radiate a dissonant or jagged energy field. When I am feeling calm, the waves around me are smooth and undisturbed. The subtle energy field that exists just surrounding my physical body sends out vibrations like electrical impulses through the air. People around me can feel my mood and level of tension.

We are all very good at nonverbal communication, whether we recognize this or not. Think of the times you have entered a gathering of people, not knowing what to expect. Do you remember how you could sense the mood in the room, the level of spontaneity or formality, of hostility or friendliness? You received this information through the airwaves, sort of the way a radar dish receives impulses from distant sources. Your senses are always scanning. And you are always sending. As the familiar saying goes, ''You can't *not* communicate.'' No matter what we are doing, even in our sleep, our bodies are radiating some kind of vibratory information reflecting our inner state.

The closer my relationship is with another, the more that person will feel and perhaps be affected by my moods, for better or for worse. If my inner feeling state changes, this is apt to be picked up immediately by my mate, and his state may change accordingly. If I become more relaxed, he may become more relaxed. As I tense up, he may do likewise.

In my graduate school training to become a psychotherapist, I was taught how to intentionally alter my state of relaxation or tension, attention or inattention, to help a client experience varying degrees of openness or anxiety. I was also taught to notice how the client's openness or resistance affected my own feeling state.

These same principles may be applied in love and work relationships. As I come to know a partner or co-worker, I come to know how that person tends to react to certain changes in me. And if I want to, I can intentionally alter my inner state to effect a desired reaction. Yet the other is still responsible for how he responds to this change in me. It's his filter that determines how he will interpret my behavior.

At first, it may have seemed paradoxical to say that I am responsible for the quality of my mood *and* you are responsible for the effect your mood has on me. But as we expand our thinking to a *both-and* perspective, the contradiction is easily accepted. We are again reminded that the interactive air space between two people is as important as the individuals themselves.

As partners become willingly responsible for how they affect each other, as they become willing to accept and able to feel how they are influencing and being influenced by each other, a sort of "sixth sense" can develop between them.

My Aunt Ida and Uncle Frank have such a relationship. If he has had a bad day at work, she can sense this before he comes home. She'll make special preparations for his arrival, putting on a fresh dress, cooking his favorite pot roast and banana cream pie. Then she will await his homecoming, ready to offer him whatever caring or attention he needs. Frank's attunement to Ida's moods is equally refined. He can sense, for example, when Ida, a former smoker, is wishing for a cigarette. At such times he will go to her and take her hand or hold her in his arms and give her a kiss. He knows that this helps to relieve her craving for a smoke and sets her mind at ease again.

Aunt Ida and Uncle Frank feel some responsibility for each other's moods. They feel how their own moods affect each other; yet they never blame each other for their own moods. Ida says she always tries to prepare herself so she feels calm and relaxed before she talks to Frank about something he has done that bothers her. Frank tells me that when he feels irritable or moody, he tries to remember to let Ida know so that she won't take it personally.

Uncle Frank and Aunt Ida are in their 70's. They did not learn these things from encounter groups or self-improvement seminars. They paid attention over the years to the exchange of energy and emotion between them and gradually they learned how to keep their love alive. They learned that when either of them is in a bad mood, this can upset both of them. Likewise, when either radiates good humor, this can help both of them feel better. They learned

also that they did not need to be the victims of each other's
low moods, that they could (usually) choose to be open to their
partner's positive influence, while letting the negative moods
pass without undue notice.

## The Paradox of Disidentification

If two people are to know and trust one another, it is
important that they be able to express feelings openly and
directly. Yet if either person becomes too emotionally
identified with or attached to his or her feelings, the
interaction can turn sour. If I am to trust your expression, I
need to feel that you really mean it. But if you seem too
attached to it, if you "mean it too much," you lose your
impact.

Often in an attempt to become dis-identified with one's
emotions (so as not to create resistance in others), people lose
touch with the vitality and immediacy of their feelings. They
become so "cool" as to appear unfeeling or insincere. This
can lead to their being ignored by others since they don't
appear to take their feelings seriously. And in fact, they don't.
This is the paradox of dis-identification: it is necessary to
express your feelings sincerely but to not take them too
seriously. Yet if you don't take them somewhat seriously,
people will feel you do not care! It is of course possible, in the
both-and world view, to both express your feelings openly and
to let the other know you are not identified with these
feelings, without indicating insincerity.

Let's look at an example of such both-and
communication:

"Honey, it hurts my feelings that you never wear the
necklace I bought you.... I have a feeling you don't
like it.... If that's true, tell me and maybe we can
exchange it for something else. Even though I'd wanted
to get you a surprise that you'd really like, I'd also
like you to have something you feel comfortable wearing.
Would you like to go shopping with me for something
else?"

This exchange shows a genuine expression of hurt feelings, a wish for feedback and a concern for the happiness of the other person. Dis-identification can leave room both for one's own feelings and the feelings of the other, without belittling either one.

## The Paradox of High Expectations

I introduce this paradox as a sort of caveat to readers of self-help books (including this one!) and participants in self-improvement programs. Reading about or working toward developing one's higher human possibilities can offer inspiration and hope. Yet it can also set up expectations that such states are easy to attain or that one ought to be more mature, thus leading to lowered self-esteem when things don't happen as expected.

I have seen couples set out on a program of marriage enrichment, only to feel more depressed and hopeless after the program than they were before. Their expectations had been raised, and they disappointed themselves. People living at poverty levels often become dissatisfied by comparing themselves to the mainstream as seen through television and magazines. When they didn't know they were "poor," they were happy. When their expectations have been raised, they can no longer be satisfied with their condition.

Anyone who sets any kind of self-improvement goal runs the risk of falling short, even if that goal is simply to become more self-accepting. (That's usually the hardest one, actually.) Yet it helps to have conscious aims and intentions in order to discover which aspects of your life you can influence and which you cannot. Having goals can contribute to disappointment, but it need not — particularly if the focus of your goal is understanding rather than control. Expectations for achieving a particular predetermined outcome are what lead to disappointment. When you can pursue your goals in a spirit of surrender, then you have succeeded in embracing paradox.

Throughout this book I will be leading you into situations which force you to confront the paradox of high expectations. I will be encouraging you to develop your capacity to think in both-and terms, when I know it is impossible to achieve that goal fully. I will be challenging you to transcend your attachment to your own point of view, while realizing that you can never see your world with complete objectivity. Yet if you can hold in mind both your wish for objectivity and the impossibility of ever fully attaining this wish, then you will not be disappointed. Once you learn to relax and face the paradox inherent in your high expectations, you can use this book as it was meant to be used — as a guide to help you feel like a winner even when things do not go as expected.

# three: What's the Struggle About?

**If you've never** experienced a power struggle, you've never been in a close human relationship. Power struggles occur between lovers, spouses, parents and children, co-workers, friends, siblings and sometimes even strangers. The more intense the emotional involvement, the greater the likelihood of struggle.

A classic power struggle involves two people fighting over the same apparently scarce resource. This scarce resource may equate to such intangibles as being right, having things done a certain way, being treated a certain way, spending time together a certain way and the like. Or the struggle may involve more tangible items such as money, time, space or fringe benefits.

Whatever the struggle appears to be about in one's relationship to the outside world, anyone who gets emotionally involved in a power struggle is also in a state of inner conflict. The power struggles between people generally mirror power struggles within. Most of us are to one degree or another at war within ourselves. Cartoonist Walt Kelly said it for all of us in Pogo's famous phrase, ''We have met the enemy, and he is us.''

The human personality is not one internally consistent whole, but a collection of traits and tendencies, some pulling the person in one direction, others tugging the opposite way. We have tendencies toward altruism and impulses toward selfishness; we feel forgiving toward ourselves at one moment and contemptuous the next; we can be full of courage or cowering in fright. Some of these qualities are quite acceptable to our images of ourselves; others we keep hidden in the shadowy recesses of our psyches. To the extent that we harbor within ourselves feelings and qualities which are denied recognition or expression, we are at war within ourselves. To this same extent, we are vulnerable to power struggles.

Frances, who has never been able to find work that she enjoys, resents the time her husband Ronald spends on his work as a research scientist. She feels a conflict within herself because of her lack of vocation, and this is reflected in her inability to accept Ronald's relationship to his work. Situations like this are as natural and normal as eating and sleeping — although more stressful! Power struggles are the growing pains of relationships.

An intense emotional relationship will call forth our inner conflicts, helping to shed light on aspects of personality which one has been unaware of or afraid to express. An emotionally engaging struggle with another person can confront us with ways of seeing and being that are new and perhaps uncomfortable. In this way we are called to stretch beyond our habitual ways of perceiving and behaving. The problem is that most of us don't stretch very easily. We have developed our personal styles over years of living. We have become identified with our own points of view and are loathe to change.

All of us see the world through the filters of our own wants, preferences, values and past experiences. The really difficult power struggles result only when you become attached to your own viewpoint as the *only* way or the *best* way, acting, perhaps unwittingly, as if you were the center of the universe.

But such behavior is so common! Where does it come from? The answer, I believe, is inexperience; neither maliciousness nor selfishness, but simple ignorance of the alternatives. Most of us have had few opportunities to experience the positive effects of seeing things from a broader perspective which includes others' views. We have been taught that differences between people are a necessary nuisance, something to be cautious about.

Our biological roots in the animal kingdom reinforce this fear of differentness. In the jungle the other was often one's predator or one's prey. We carry with us, both in our collective consciousness and in our collective unconscious, the tendency to feel threatened by whomever we define as "other." Thus threatened or insecure in our position, we naturally cling to it more tightly.

## We're All Different

People differ in the ways they like it served.

Some like life on a silver platter. Others prefer to hunt it and fix it themselves. Some feel nervous when there's not enough on their plates. Others get anxious when their plates are too full.

People who felt loved and wanted as children tend to see the world as warm and welcoming. People who felt rejected or ignored often see the world as a cold, unfriendly, or at best neutral, place. One's early experiences contribute heavily to one's later perceptions.

"It all depends on your perspective," say the contemporary philosophers. How you look and how much you can see determine how you will interpret the events of your life. Looking at events with squinted, critical eyes affords one impression; softly-focused wide eyes yield quite a different view. Focusing on only one point of view tends to strengthen belief in that point of view; attending two or more viewpoints simultaneously allows recognition that each has partial validity. Some of us have an easier time than others embracing new and different points of view.

## But Is It Safe To Be Different?

"He's different."

"She's different."

The very term "different" implies something a bit strange or odd. Most people strive for normality and feel perhaps a little ashamed of any obvious differentness. If you've ever been in any kind of support group, such as a women's or men's group or a single parents' group, you've probably observed how relieved people often feel when they find out, "I'm not the only one with these fears and insecurities...I'm not so different after all!"

Why do people seem to fear their differentness, their uniqueness of experience and perspective? Why do we so often avoid standing alone? While the roots of this fear of differentness may lie deep in our collective psyche, there is another side to the fears of most people. The soul also longs to express its uniqueness, its one-and-only gift to the collective human drama. We wish to express ourselves in our own ways, yet we fear that our ways may not be seen as valid or worthy of respect. Some of us overcome this dilemma by becoming authorities about something or other, thus managing to avoid some of the insecurity. But most of us struggle to be heard, and hopefully respected, every day of our lives.

Another element which contributes to power struggles is a lesson most of us learn early in life: *If my way is valid and right, your way must be wrong. Either* your perspective is valid *or* mine is. Both cannot be. This same sort of either-or thinking causes our struggles within ourselves. Somehow we get the idea that a strong person cannot show weakness; one who is ambitious cannot also be lazy; one who is self-assured cannot feel insecure. Thus, we say yes to perhaps one half of our personal potential and no to the other half.

I read in the newspaper this morning a story about a killing. Two men in a videogame arcade got into a quarrel. One shot and killed the other. Two witnesses on the scene gave conflicting accounts of the incident: one said the man who did the killing provoked the argument; the other said he shot in self-defense. Could both be right? Entertaining the possibility that both views are correct plays havoc with our current legal and judicial systems. Most people have grown accustomed to a mind-set which allows room for only one right answer or one winner: multiple-choice tests in school and professional certification exams; our adversary legal system; our culture's most popular sports; beauty contests and contests of all kinds. When we adopt this mind-set, others become our competitors in the race to be right or best.

You may say that you have outgrown this mentality, that it no longer exerts the same influence in your life as it once did. Perhaps this is so. Yet we live in a culture which is just beginning to question this mentality and to search for new ways of seeing things. Thus, it is impossible to live entirely independent of such an attitude, even though you yourself don't believe in it anymore. Or do you?

There is a famous Sufi teaching story about three blind men who encountered an elephant as they walked down the road one day. The first blind man came upon the elephant's side and asserted to his companions, "The road ends here. We have come to a wall." The second bumped into one of the elephant's legs, wrapped his arms around it, and protested, "No, it is only a tree." A moment later the third blind man came into contact with the elephant's tail and assured his cohorts, "It most certainly is nothing but a rope." This story tends to disrupt a belief in either-or approaches to interpreting reality. Humanity as a whole is very much like those three blind men, each clinging to a little piece of the truth, ignoring how that piece might fit with those of others, fighting for the right to be right.

I find myself being somewhat secretive about my own differentness. Perhaps if I let others see my most cherished views, they will try to talk me into abandoning my way in favor of theirs. Where did such a fear come from in me? I suspect it came from growing up in an if-I'm-right-you're-wrong either-or culture. As a child I learned to watch out for the big people because they were always telling me what was and wasn't so, regardless of whether this agreed with my experience. The big people assumed that they had the power to validate or invalidate the perceptions of the little people. Most of them seemed to think that this was their job!

Big-people power has been institutionalized in almost every culture on the globe. It goes by the name of education. As youngsters, we are educated in how to interpret, conceptualize and categorize our uniquely personal experiences. As a result, we all come out of the schools seeing things more or less the same as everyone else, or at least pretending that we do.

So far in this chapter, I've offered two reasons why people fear being different from one another:

—    It is popularly believed that if I'm right, that makes someone else wrong; either I'm a threat to him or he's a threat to me. This leaves our whole relationship with one another on a pretty insecure foundation.

—    Most people remember what it was like to be a little person in a world dominated by big people. The big folks seemed to see it as their duty, when the little ones expressed themselves, to correct the immature perceptions. Thus, to show my differentness, my unique point, angle or range of view, is to open myself to a possible power struggle, and one which I might very well lose.

Yet struggle can stimulate growth and change. Through the confrontation of two different ways something new is created. If I live in isolation from other people, my viewpoint is never challenged and forced to expand. While I fear your differentness, I also need it to stay alive and growing.

To find harmony in this crazy world, we need to develop the capacity to embrace paradox. We need to recognize both the inevitability of conflict between people and the possibility of harmony through coming to value and understand conflict. The surprising thing about differences is that the more you try to hide, overlook or otherwise avoid facing them, the more pain they cause. Differences are inevitable. If you assume that should not be so, you are likely to experience more unhappiness than if you could simply allow the differences to exist and start from there.

Likewise, if you believe your personality should be totally consistent, leaving no room for the expression of apparently opposing or contradictory impulses, you will become more and more your own worst enemy. Life is a painful battle when you struggle against the inevitable. And differences among people, in wants and perceptions, are inevitable facts of life. We create power struggles when we cannot openly and respectfully accept our differences from others and the contradictory impulses within ourselves.

## License for Lunacy

When I was a youngster of about 11, I read Bertrand Russell's autobiography in which he described, among other things, his life goals and values. A passage that made a deep impression on me during those formative years was one in which he disclosed that he had lived his entire life in a manner that would afford him a "license for lunacy." To Russell, possessing a license for lunacy meant that people would leave you alone or perhaps even respect you when you did things that might ordinarily be considered odd or deviant. It was a license to do your own thing, to be free of others' attempts at control. Russell achieved this by becoming a highly respected philospher and mathematician. He felt he had to make it publicly clear that his lifework was dedicated to the social good in order to be allowed to be a social "deviant" in other ways; for example, an atheist.

How many of us wish, as Russell did, for the freedom to express ourselves in our own way? Any how many of us feel we have to fight constantly to maintain this freedom?

The struggle for freedom of expression and self-determination seems to be a global theme, not simply a personal one, during this time in human history. The power struggles that frequent our significant love and work relationships are microcosmic mirrors of the struggles which ravage our planet.

How difficult it is for us to see the world, politically and ideologically, from any viewpoint different from the one we hold. We can't imagine how others can be so narrow-minded!

And so it is at a personal level. We can't fully open to each other as cultures and nations for the same reasons we can't open to each other as lovers, spouses, friends and co-workers. We are afraid; in the either-or world which we now inhabit, the presence of any other viewpoint is a threat to our own.

As if our personal fears and defenses were not enough, we must also deal with human organizations based on the either-or attitude. Organizations are structured to turn a profit with a limited amount of capital and human resources. Different departments within an organization must compete for the same funds; individuals compete against one another for jobs and promotions. If Tom and Dick represent different departments in competition for the same resources, they will tend to see things in terms of their own departmental interests. Likewise, if Juan has just landed a position that Ted wanted, Ted may have a hard time feeling supportive of the company's affirmative action program.

A typical manufacturing organization is divided into such functions as production, marketing, and quality control. A division that is charged with generating markets and sales for a product may be less concerned with the product's quality than with meeting sales quotas. The quality control people see things differently. Their aim is to maintain certain standards; they may send back to the assembly line any widgets which do not measure up. This can fuel the fires of misunderstanding between the three functions: marketing has to keep sales up; quality control is slowing down production by sending back widgets; production feels caught in the squeeze. In addition, each separate segment will compete against the others for its budget or to protect its interests. This leaves most organizations at war within their own ranks.

There are signs on the horizon, however, that point to a world-wide transformation, a shift away from the whole notion of win-lose, right-wrong, either-you-or-me, either-this-or-that. Let me summarize just a few of these trends:

- General Motors, Alcoa, and other industries are beginning to use cross-division teams for everything from R&D to marketing of their new products. GM's new Saturn car is being developed, manufactured, and marketed by teams which include representatives from R&D, Manufacturing, Marketing, Quality Control, and all other concerned divisions. This promotes a spirit of cooperative, both-and problem solving, rather than either-or internal competition.

- In the branch of physics called quantum mechanics, it had for many years been debated whether electromagnetic energy was composed of discrete individual *particles* or of pattern-forming *waves*. In the last 20 years, the consistent evidence that electromagnetic phenomena exhibit *both* particle *and* wave properties has led physicists to work toward a theory which encompasses both perspectives.

- In our social relations, we are seeing a blurring of either-or sex-role stereotyped behavior and expectations for men and women. Both women and men are engaging in pastimes and occupations formerly thought to be the domain of the other sex, while at the same time doing all the things generally considered typical for their own sex. Thus, I might both make curtains for my kitchen and repair my car in a typical day, without feeling unusual or deviant.

- In the popular media, we are seeing the increased usage of such both-and terms and phrases as: *androgyny*, uniting the characteristics of both male and female or flexibly expressing both masculine and feminine qualities; *gentle persuasion*, blending both the will to power and respect for feelings; *high tech/high touch*, a term used in industry to emphasize the importance of balancing the material wonders of technology with the spiritual demands of our human nature.

- There is a movement in the field of athletics which questions the value of winners and losers. Out of this movement have come such innovations as Zen tennis, inner skiing, New Games and Playfair. Each of these innovations represents a type of non-competitive athletics, where the experience of the game is valued over winning.
- In the field of family law, more and more attorneys are discovering the pitfalls of the adversary legal system when applied to a divorcing family unit. Many lawyers are taking advanced training in mediation skills so that they can act as objective third-party family mediators in divorce cases, rather than as advocates for one side of the family against the other.

The institution of ''no-fault'' divorce in many states is further evidence of this change in the legal system's view of the complexities of marital conflict.

- In a similar vein, most insurance companies now offer no-fault automobile insurance policies to drivers, recognizing that in most auto accidents, it is difficult to assign fault to just one person.
- Our culture's bookshelves and popular media are full of topics relating to the meeting of Eastern and Western ways of thought. Books like *The Tao of Physics* and films like ''Ghandi'' illustrate a movement toward the wedding of things formerly thought to be separate, or in an either-or relationship to one another, such as outer material progress and inner spiritual development; science and mysticism; activism and pacifism.

## The Meeting of Eastern and Western Medicine

One idea from the ancient Eastern traditions which is infiltrating the Western mind is the idea of the seven vital energy centers, or chakras, in the human body. According to the Eastern chakra system, a ''map'' of the human energy system, the human body houses seven energy centers, aligned from the base of the spine to the top of the head. Each chakra energy center is related to the function of a specific endocrine gland or nerve plexus, and each is associated with a specific personal or spiritual quality.

The first chakra, at the base of the spine, is concerned with individual physical survival. The second, just below the navel, is associated with species survival, reproduction and sexuality. The third, at the solar plexus (near the diaphragm) is the center dealing with power relationships and power struggles. The fourth, near the heart, determines one's capacity for compassion or love. The fifth, at the throat, deals with self-expression and creativity. The sixth, at the center of the forehead, houses one's capacity for intuition, inner sight and objectivity. The seventh chakra, at the top of the head, concerns one's openness to an attitude of unity with all creation.

According to this map of the human energy system, any chakra may be open, with the ability to exchange energy freely with the environment, or closed, to a greater or lesser degree. When a person's sexual center, for example, is open, that person has the capacity to use sexual energy appropriately. To the extent that it is closed, the person's sexual response may be blocked or expressed compulsively or inappropriately.

As one matures or evolves personally and spiritually, one masters the ability to remain open at the higher centers and to function at higher levels without shutting down one's lower centers. Thus, with maturation, one becomes able to express love (chakra four) without giving up one's power (chakra three), or to express critical truths (chakra five) without sacrificing love or compassion. Personal evolution is seen as an ever-widening expansion of one's capacities, as a process characterized by "both...and...and this too."

The chakra centers which are of most concern in these times for most people seem to be the third and the fourth, the power center and the love center. As individuals, as men and women, and as nations, we now face the developmental task of learning to express both power and love simultaneously. The cultural stage is set for such a transformation. Our minds are being prepared for a shift in our mind-set. But so far, in our personal lives, most of us still manage to "hurt the ones we love," as the famous 1940's song title laments.

Our fear may be that if we center our awareness on the fourth chakra, we will lose our power, our hard-won capacity to use our third chakra energy; if we open our hearts to another in love, we may feel somehow in a one-down position. Most of us have never in our lives experienced the rewards that occur when we are truly open-hearted and trusting. We remember the times we have opened ourselves a little and been burned, so we continue to protect ourselves.

We know or intuit that there is a more expanded, more open way of being than the one to which we have become accustomed. We think of the lives of Christ, Ghandhi, Martin Luther King, Jr. Yet these men were martyrs, killed before the natural ending of their lives, presumably because they threatened the existing order. Are our fears justified?

In international relations, it is even harder to be open and trusting. Our national defense systems, and those of other nations, are designed to instill feelings of fear in one's adversaries. According to the rules of the international diplomacy game, one must appear tough if one is to avoid being dominated by other nations.

Up until now, then, to open one's fourth chakra fully has meant pain or threat or even death. Why should we believe it will be any different in the future? The truth of course is, we never know. It is always a risk. But today's world is making the risks of the power-without-love approach equally apparent: the dangers of nuclear weapons proliferation; the unhappy marriages which result when one spouse dominates the other; the low employee morale and productiivity which occurs when workers feel used by their bosses.

The problem up to now has been that the world was not ready for a *both* power *and* love approach to resolving conflicts. Our either-or way of thinking has predisposed us to see people (and nations) as aggressive (powerful) or naive (loving). We have few public models which combine power and love in a strong yet open way of relating. We are accustomed to seeing good people pitted against bad people, civilized people against barbarians, enlightened people against misguided people. And so the stage has been set for one religious war after another, both nationally and in our personal lives.

The time has come for the human species to make a collective shift from a third chakra to a fourth chakra attitude, toward an attitude that includes all views as having some validity yet which does not give absolute power to any one way. Admittedly, humanity has a long way to go before we can consistently embrace such an attitude in relation to strangers or our "enemies." We can, however, begin to learn ways of being powerfully loving and lovingly powerful in our daily love lives and work lives. Our lovers, spouses, friends and co-workers *want* to trust and respect us. And even then we have problems! But it makes sense to start learning about how to get beyond power struggles at the places where most of us spend most of our time — at home and at work.

## The Importance of a Good Fight

While the either-or attitude that engenders power struggles is something to be outgrown, most relationships pass through a stage where such struggle is necessary and healthy. Most relationships also wax and wane to some extent between the adversarial, either-or, and the cooperative, both-and, mind-set.

In the model of relationships presented in *The Couple's Journey*, derived from interviews with over 100 couples, the Power Struggle Stage usually occurs after the Romance Stage. (Actually it is the second of five stages I have described in detail in that book: Romance, Power Struggle, Stability, Commitment, Co-Creation.) This stage is a time for opening up communication about doubts, fears, disappointments, resentments and resistances about one another or the relationship. It is a time for fully exploring differences and one's feelings about these differences.

Just as it is natural during the Romance Stage to focus on similarities and compatibilities, during the Power Struggle Stage it is natural to look at the other side of the coin. And this is true whether we are talking about love relationships or work relationships. In the world of work, for example, one often enters a new job, new supervisory relationship or new partnership with optimism and high hopes. After a time, however, the normal difficulties of collaboration and compromise become apparent. It becomes clear that if you are to work together effectively, certain differences or difficulties need to be resolved.

The Power Struggle Stage is temporary but necessary in most relationships. It occurs as a way of testing and building trust. Perhaps if people were naturally more trusting and less alienated from each other, power struggles would not be necessary. But most people cannot sustain a feeling of complete trust through the difficulties that normally occur in close love or work relationships. We may live together in harmony for long periods, but should a major disagreement occur, our trust may be shaken for a time and need to be tested and rebuilt. Thus, we must learn to accept our need to fight for our rights on occasion as an aspect of the growth of the relationship.

Many people think they can get through life without ever facing an interpersonal struggle. In their love lives, these people have a common pattern: one romantic relationship after another or several at once. In their work lives, they move from job to job, or find a niche where they can remain invisible. Many wish to avoid struggle, but we know that we must occasionally fight to have our points of view heard and respected. It is your responsibility, if you are trying to build a relationship with someone, to do whatever is necessary to help that person understand you. This may mean that you have to repeat yourself over and over. It may mean you have to speak more forcefully than you are comfortable with. It may mean that you will have to show strong or tender feelings that you don't usually show to anyone.

The function of the Power Struggle Stage of relationships is to really come to know each other in all your various aspects. If there are parts of you that you feel unable to express in the relationship, you need to test the limits. Find out if these aspects of your being are really unacceptable to your partner or if you are being unnecessarily timid. Testing the limits of a relationship is a way to discover its true depth. If it turns out that many of your most cherished traits and feelings are unacceptable to the other person, then it may be time to end the relationship or to significantly redefine its meaning in your life. It is better to find this out than to continue with a veneer of harmony covering your fear and anger about not being free to express yourself.

The Power Struggle Stage is a time for expanding the boundaries of a relationship, a time for bringing the formerly hidden aspects of both people into full view — particularly those aspects that you imagine may threaten the relationship. As you come to care for someone more or develop a closer working relationship, you often come to feel new parts of yourself, new feelings or traits, pressing for expression. Sometimes these parts feel threatening or even destructive to the relationship. Yet the urge for integrity, for wholeness, causes them to seek expression.

Penelope Prentice is a friend of mine. During the courtship phases of each of her three marriages (over a span of 25 years), Penelope was never able to express to her fiance her doubts about whether he was the right man for her to marry. She was so addicted to pleasing men and so afraid of ''wrecking the romance,'' that she hid these very important feelings from her partner and pretended that everything was all right. During the year before her third marriage, she entered psychotherapy in order to deal with this issue. But all she was able to do in therapy was to gain insight into her pattern. She wasn't able to change it. She could express her doubts about marriage to her therapist but not to her husband-to-be. As a result, she never felt really committed during the ensuing years of marriage. The doubts nagged her constantly. Yet she couldn't bring herself to clear the air. She held on as long as she could but eventually sought divorce as the only way of escape from her doubts and resistances.

At age 50, Penelope found herself in a relationship where she was able to express to her partner her doubts about him and her resistances to intimacy in general. She was able to say, "I'm not ready yet to make a commitment to you," instead of pretending to be madly in love. Remarkably, paradoxically, when she was able to do this she felt more in love than she ever had before. The romance became more passionate for both Penelope and her partner; yet they were both more honest than they'd ever been before about their doubts and fears.

This is a strong testament to the importance of giving the power struggle its due. Since you probably can't avoid it, you'd best learn to embrace it. Penelope escaped it for 50 years, but it finally caught up with her. Life seems to be like that. Whatever you try hardest to avoid will get you sooner or later.

Not everyone will identify with the story of Penelope Prentice. Some people avoid harmony, compulsively disagreeing "whether they want to or not," just as Penelope was compulsively agreeable. Some people can't tell another person what they want or like, either because they are ashamed of it or because they don't know it themselves. Each of us has something in ourselves that we habitually avoid expressing or revealing. Whatever this something is in your case, it will press for expression — or at least recognition — at a certain stage in all your significant relationships. If you avoid it, you may avoid a power struggle for the time being, but it will follow you throughout your life. If you risk expressing it in a relationship, there is a chance that the relationship will be lost. But there is also a chance that the relationship will be deepened and strengthened beyond what you thought possible.

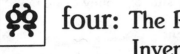 **four:** The Polar Dimensions Inventory

**This chapter is** a reader participation activity, the Polar Dimensions Inventory, designed to guide you in a systematic look at your own behavior. It's an opportunity to learn more about yourself and your characteristic style of doing things.

Why are people initially attracted to one another? Why do people of different types have difficulty understanding each other? The Inventory, although not a validated "psychological test," can help partners and co-workers understand their similarities and differences. Your answers to the items may vary during different periods of your life and in different relationships or situations.

As you answer the questions, it is best to hold in mind a particular relationship with another person. If possible, make a copy of the questionnaire for your friend/partner, and complete your answers at the same time (but separately!). Then compare your results in light of the discussion in the chapter which follows.

Circle the letter to the left of the statement that is most true of you most of the time. Scoring instructions are given at the end of the Inventory.

1. Would you rather...with a large sum of money given to you?
    a. make a profitable investment
    b. buy a new wardrobe

2. If you are to be married, do you prefer...?
    a. a large elegant wedding and dinner reception for your friends and family
    b. a small simple ceremony and reception

3. On your vacation, would you rather...?
    a. get a motel with kitchen facilities so you can cook most of your own meals
    b. eat in fine restaurants and sleep in plush hotels

4. When you move to a new city, are you more likely to...?
    a. sell or give away many of your belongings and buy new things when you get relocated
    b. bring everything with you

5. When ordering from a restaurant menu, do you...?
    a. choose what you like regardless of price
    b. carefully consider prices before choosing

6. When travelling to a distant land, would you rather...?
    a. sail
    b. fly

7. Are you...?
    a. always on time, sometimes even early, for appointments
    b. usually a little late

8. Are you more likely to do a job...?
    a. quickly, but not quite thoroughly
    b. slowly and carefully

9. When you have free time, are you more likely to spend it...?
    a. working on a project
    b. dreaming of a project

10. Do work schedules and deadlines...?
    a. cause resistance in you
    b. seem a matter of course

11. When you and your partner have free time around the house, would you rather...?
    a. work on your own separate projects in separate but adjacent rooms
    b. spend time cuddling or talking together

12. With your partner, would you rather talk about...?
    a. the kids or relatives
    b. your relationship

13. Do you prefer to be given a compliment...?
    a. directly, to your face
    b. behind your back, but so that it gets back to you

14. Upon arriving home from work, do you prefer...?
    a. a period of quiet alone time
    b. a time of sharing with your partner the events of the day

15. In going to a restaurant with your partner, do you like to be seated...?
    a. so that you can both see the view or other people
    b. facing each other

16. In deciding whether to take a new job, do you place more weight on...?
    a. an assessment of pros and cons
    b. your overall gut feeling

17. In looking back over the love relationships you have had in your life (or almost had), do you tend to choose partners who...?
    a. feel right or necessary in some unexplainable way
    b. make sense for you to be with, based on somewhat objective criteria

18. In making a case for your point of view, do you...?
    a. use stories and anecdotes that speak to people's feelings
    b. use logic, data or straightforward common sense

19. When solving a complex technical problem, do you...?
    a. systematically plan and carry out your approach, consulting experts and references where necessary
    b. operate mostly on intuitions, feelings and hunches, trusting your past experience to guide you when necessary

20. When someone insults you, do you...?
    a. think about what caused the person to behave that way
    b. react with hurt or anger

21. When someone whom you trust offers you an investment opportunity, are you more likely to...?
    a. go for it if it seems sound
    b. check and re-check the facts, inferences and sources

22. Would you rather climb a mountain...?
    a. using existing trails
    b. by carving out a new trail

23. In giving feedback to a co-worker about her work, would you be more likely to...?
   a. first find out how she is feeling
   b. tell her what you think or feel first

24. If you want to make love, and you're not sure if your partner is receptive, do you...?
   a. approach amorously
   b. hint around about how you are feeling

25. In learning a new skill, would you rather...?
   a. be placed in a real situation where you are forced to use the skill
   b. wait until you are proficient before applying it in a real life situation.

26. Would you rather...?
   a. listen to an interesting speech
   b. deliver an interesting speech

27. Would you rather...?
   a. direct the work of others, even if some of them resist your direction
   b. be given direction from someone you respect

28. In conversations with your partner, do you spend more time...?
   a. talking
   b. listening

29. In relationship to your partner or co-worker, are you more likely to...?
   a. make decisions and set directions
   b. support or carry out directions and goals set by your partner

30. Would you rather...?
     a. have your ideas supported by others
     b. be supportive of others' ideas

31. Would you rather be...?
     a. closing an important business deal
     b. hanging out in bed with your lover

32. As a birthday present, would you prefer to receive...?
     a. tickets to a professional sports event
     b. a "gift certificate" for a massage from a loved one

33. When you open up the newspaper, are you more likely to turn first to...?
     a. funnies or human interest features
     b. business, finance or world affairs

34. If you could be assured success in anything you wanted, would you rather be...?
     a. president of your own company
     b. a musician, artist or writer

35. When you have free time to do anything you wish, are you more likely to...?
     a. do something that makes you feel good
     b. do something for self-improvement

## Scoring the Polar Dimensions Inventory

The scoring process sounds a bit complex at first; it's not. You'll compare your answer on each question to the keys below, then sum up your scores to see how you compare with the characteristics of each of the seven polar dimensions. Here's how:

Give yourself one point each time your answer corresponds to the letter listed in the key for that dimension. Your score for the first-mentioned dimension is simply the total of those points. For the second-mentioned dimension, just subtract your first score from 5.

Maybe your answers on items 1 through 5, the Saver-Spender dimension, looked like this:

    1. a
    2. b
    3. a
    4. a
    5. b

Here's the key for the *Saver-Spender* dimension. Give yourself one point on your "saver" score each time your answer matches the key.

*Saver*
    1. a
    2. b
    3. a
    4. b
    5. b

Matching your hypothetical answers to the key, "your" Saver (first-mentioned dimension) score would be 4 (four matches with the key), and "your" Spender score, 1 (5 - 4). Thus, "you" tend to be more of a Saver than a Spender.

In the next chapter I'll describe each of these polar dimensions more fully. For now, here are the rest of the dimension keys:

Key for items 6 — 10, the *Scurrier-Dawdler* polarity
    *Scurrier*
    6. b
    7. b
    8. a
    9. a
    10. b

Key for items 11 — 15, the *Parallel-Face to Face* polarity
    *Parallel*
    11. a
    12. a
    13. b
    14. a
    15. a

Key for items 16 — 20, the *Thinker-Feeler* polarity
    *Thinker*
    16. a
    17. b
    18, b
    19. a
    20. a

Key for items 21 — 25, the *Leaper-Looker* polarity
    *Leaper*
    21. a
    22. b
    23. b
    24. a
    25. a

Key for items 26 — 30, the *Space Maker-Space Taker* polarity
    *Space Maker*
    26. a
    27. b
    28. b
    29. b
    30. b

Key for items 31 — 35, the *Lover-Warrior* polarity
   *Lover*
   31. b
   32. b
   33. a
   34. b
   35. a

Write down your scores and those of your partner on each of the polar dimensions, and identify the dimension which best describes your respective styles on each scale. Are you a Spender or a Saver, a Thinker or a Feeler, a Warrior or a Lover? How about your partner? In the next chapter we'll take a look at the meaning of these results.

# five: Attraction, Polarization, Reconciliation

Smith likes to be given a difficult assignment and then be left alone with it. Jones prefers to give his workers a lot of encouragement and direction, so they feel a part of his team.

Shirley likes to make love in the early evening, sometimes taking hours for caressing and sharing sweet intimacies. Fred likes to make love late at night and go right to sleep afterward.

On their European vacation, Sid wanted to go first class, eating in the best restaurants and staying in luxury hotels. Martha hated to waste their money on such frills. She preferred to go economy class, staying in youth hostels and buying their meals in grocery stores.

Whenever two people get together for any purpose, their differences soon become apparent. And even though the two may be both similar and different in many ways, usually one particular area of difference will cause more stress than their other differences. This area of difference will generally arise only after they have known each other for quite a while. But once it has arisen, the two parties involved often center all of their power struggles around this key dimension, at least for a time.

## Antagonistic and Complementary Differences

There are many ways in which two people may differ from each other. Some differences are easily accepted. Others become a basis for struggle. The differences which lead to struggle are usually those around which both partners have some emotional sensitivity, be it conscious or unconscious. Often power struggles center on some polar opposite characteristic, which leads the two to behave or see things 180 degrees differently from one another.

For example, one person may desire a life of comfort and security, while the other craves adventure and change. Ironically, it often occurs that the same set of polar characteristics that lead to struggle were at one time a major source of *attraction* between the two people! A man may be attracted to a woman's love of adventure, only to find later on that he can never get her to stay at home. Or she may be initially drawn to his solid reliability, only to be disillusioned when she realizes how rigid and unyielding he is.

Attraction can turn into repulsion. If a couple's complementary polarities become rigidly polarized, the differences that once beguiled and bewitched become sources of misunderstanding. Partners may begin to emphasize and exaggerate their differences in ways which feel punishing or antagonistic. As this polarization process proceeds, partners may forget what it was that drew them together and lose contact with their earlier feelings of attraction.

Such a polarization or growing apart can be reconciled if partners can step outside or above the struggle in order to view it from a greater distance. If partners can see the polar dimension along which their struggle is being played out, it can help them to understand that each one's behavior represents one side of a two-sided coin.

The attraction-polarization-reconciliation process is a

frequent and familiar cycle in both love and work relationships. To illustrate this phenomenon, and to give you some feedback on the questionnaire you completed in the previous chapter, here is the description I promised of the seven common polarities that create struggle among couples and co-workers:

— the Saver vs. the Spender
— the Scurrier vs. the Dawdler
— the Parallel Player vs. the Face to Face Player
— the Lover vs. the Warrior
— the Space Taker vs. the Space Maker
— the Looker vs. the Leaper
— the Thinker vs. the Feeler.

As you read the seven descriptions, remember that each pole represents a somewhat consistent style of behavior; yet most people have the potential for behaving in either style — or anywhere between the two poles. Even so, couple relationships often bring out people's oppositeness — an interesting and somewhat puzzling phenomenon. I offer these polar types as an introduction to the notion of polarities and as a way of illustrating the process of attraction, polarization, and reconciliation. In reality, of course, there are no pure types; no one fits into any category exactly!

## The Saver and the Spender

In the eyes of the Saver, the resources of the world are limited, which leads to an attitude of conservation and thriftiness.

To the Spender, resources are abundant and plentiful. Thus, there is no need to think about conserving for the future.

To the objective eye, both positions are part true and part false. But in relationships, we are dealing not so much with facts as with feelings. When the Spender orders an after-dinner drink and dessert, after what the Saver feels is an already expensive and over-filling meal, the Saver sits in the corner with a worried frown. When the Saver wants to stay home and watch television instead of going out and paying for a movie, the Spender feels deprived.

Spenders buy now and pay later.

Savers put things away for a rainy day.

Spenders tend to live beyond their means. Savers live beneath their means.

Spenders are often generous, both with themselves and with others, even if they don't quite have the resources to back up such generosity.

Savers are often frugal, both with themselves and others. But they generally tend to have something in the bank to fall back on...just in case.

Often when the Spender runs out of cash, he will turn to the Saver, who is sure to have something in reserve. This, of course, reinforces the Saver's belief that conservation pays; for if she didn't have that nest egg stashed away, what would become of the Spender?

In my own family tree, the men have always been the Spenders and women the Savers. Both of my grandmothers worked hard and saved frugally in order to support their husbands' more extravagant lifestyles and habits.

My maternal grandmother Lil Brooks, a competent and talented woman born in 1875, married my grandfather Wilson Brooks, a housebuilder and fiddle-player, when she was just 17. She was attracted by his generosity and his dramatic flair. He was attracted by her integrity and her guts. After a time, Wilson became less and less interested in housebuilding, the occupation by which he earned a living, and more and more attracted to fiddling, a creative outlet which also afforded him many opportunities for socializing and spending money on food and drink. This meant to Lil that it was now up to her to provide for the two of them and their six small children.

And so their roles were cast. She became the keeper of the purse-strings. He continued to fiddle and spend. As she became more conservative, he became more outrageous in his spending, drink-buying and gift-giving. Each grew to see the other as an opponent, as someone whose values and ways went against one's own. They were in a power struggle. From the stories they told me, it wasn't easy, but they never questioned their life's circumstances. They simply lived out their struggle stoically until they died.

Although times have changed, the dynamics of Saver-Spender relationships are as they have always been, except for one crucial difference: there is now more social support for communicating openly about difficult emotions. Nowadays, we are exposed — via television, magazines, books and educational seminars — to a variety of models for frank self-expression. Now we are more apt to step back from our emotional reactions, to see them as just that, emotional reactions, and to talk about our feelings in ways that can help us get unhooked from our unquestioning, mechanical approach to life.

If the Saver is able to communicate her point of view to the Spender, without blame, defensiveness or self-righteousness, the Spender, and in the process the Saver herself, will become more accepting of this style of doing things. Before long, when he does not feel the threat of being backed into a corner, the Spender may come to feel inside himself certain Saver-like qualities. If he can't depend on the Saver to look over his shoulder to make sure he doesn't overspend, he may have to begin to police himself, in the process becoming more aware of his own conservative tendencies.

If the Saver can relax and accept some of her own Spender tendencies, it becomes even more likely that the Spender will grow in his acceptance of his Saver qualities. As she accepts her other side, she becomes more accepting of him. In turn, he can become more accepting, both of her and of the side of himself which is like her — his conservative, thrifty side.

In communicating an attitude of acceptance, the Saver might begin by disclosing how it feels to be her kind of person:

"Darling, I want you to know what it feels like inside of me when you come home after a shopping trip with a new suit and a couple of new pairs of shoes. I get this 'what about me?' feeling — sort of like when I was a little girl and my parents always bought more stuff for my younger sister because she always *asked* for more. And me, I was the good girl who never bothered my parents with a lot of wants. And now of course my habit of not asking and not spending on myself continues. But it still causes me pain to have that situation brought back to me.

"There's another side to it too, though. I like that I'm able to exist on very little. And I like that I try to consume only what I really need.

"I know that you and I have developed different habits for spending money. But maybe we need to step back from our usual way of doing things. Just because we've always done things a certain way doesn't mean it's the only way...What do you think?"

The conversation that ensues from an opening like this is apt to be characterized by two-way discussion, self-disclosure, trust, and mutual respect, as a result of the tone that has already been set.

Either the Saver or the Spender can initiate such a conversation. Whoever makes the first move sets the stage — for dialogue or for struggle. From the Saver's remarks above, we can discern some of the essential ingredients of power struggle-resolving, or dialogue-enhancing, communication:

— She started from an attitude of feeling and expressing her connectedness to him.

— She opened to him some of her softer, little-girl feelings. (Sharing these is almost never threatening to the other since they can see clearly that they are not the cause of such feelings.)

— She expressed both sides of her feelings rather than making herself *either* a victim *or* totally in control of her feelings. (Either extreme tends to push the other away.)

— She supported his right to be different from her.

— She challenged both him and herself to re-examine their pattern in a way that implied shared responsibility rather than, "it's your problem."

— She expressed her viewpoint and then asked for his, giving him time to respond. This communicates that she not only wants to be heard, but that she also wants to listen, to know and understand him.

In describing my grandparents, I implied that Savers and Spenders are often attracted to each other because they each want what the other has. After a time, as we have seen before, attraction turns to polarization as each side struggles against the other in a fight to be recognized or to "be oneself." As we know, "being oneself" can be self-limiting as well as expanding. If the Saver fights for the freedom to be herself by defending against recognizing the part of her that wishes to spend more freely, then she is limiting the expression of her full self. She may never become as relaxed about money as her Spender partner, but if she can at least own up to her Spender tendencies, she has found a way to use the relationship as a vehicle for deepening her relationship to herself.

## The Scurrier and the Dawdler

Like the Saver and the Spender, the Scurrier and the Dawdler often hate each other for the same qualities they once loved in each other. At first one is attracted to a quality that he or she needs to learn about; we all have an inner drive toward wholeness or self-knowledge. This may account for the sense of mystery that often accompanies the romance stage of a relationship. The quality which attracts or fascinates may be unfamiliar in one's own experience.

After a time, however, this same unfamiliarity can be the basis for difficulties in understanding one another. This may result in mutual irritation, a tendency to blame the other for causing friction, or attempts to change each other. Partners find themselves resisting each other and defending against the other's perceived attacks. They may become quite inflexible and entrenched in their positions, leading to the condition called polarization.

The Scurrier sees life as a race against the clock. He often has too much to do and not enough time in which to do it. This can cause him to feel anxious much of the time. Yet deep inside, most Scurriers long for relaxation and freedom from schedules. This accounts for his initial attraction to the Dawdler's more relaxed way of moving through the world.

The Dawdler sees life as a journey, not a destination. Dawdlers appear at times to have nowhere to go, to have little sense of purpose or ambition. Yet within their hearts they are as concerned as anyone else to make their contribution to the world. Sensing in themselves some wavering and doubt about their life purpose and direction, Dawdlers can find Scurriers' apparent sense of direction quite attractive, at least at first.

Later in the relationship, whether in love or at work, as intimate knowledge grows and illusions fade, each tends to notice the other side of the partner's coin. If the Scurrier is camouflaging a wavering sense of purpose behind his high activity level, then the Dawdler has a good vantage point from which to observe this, being only too conscious of her *own* wavering sense of direction.

If the Dawdler is covering a high anxiety level behind a veneer of calm relaxation, then the Scurrier will certainly sense this, being himself quite attuned to anxiety-based behavior.

The power struggle begins when partners become rigidly polarized around some dimension of difference, instead of relating to their differences as reflecting a dynamic, ever-changing *polarity*; in other words, instead of recognizing that *sometimes* he's anxious and *sometimes* he's calm, sometimes she scurries and sometimes she takes her time, they *polarize* themselves and each other into fixed, rigid categories: she is *the* Dawdler, and he is *the* Scurrier.

In work settings, the Scurrier-Dawdler polarity often gets played out in connection with deadlines. When it comes to meeting a prearranged (and often dictated-from-above) timetable, different people have different styles or habits. At work, however, it is common for the get-it-done-on-time Scurriers to feel righteous about their particular habit, since this style has obvious rewards in most work settings. The more laid back Dawdler types are often seen as hard to manage, or even as having an authority problem.

The fireworks begin when a Scurrier boss has to delegate a piece of important work to a Dawdler subordinate. Assuming the two have had an ongoing work relationship, we can easily imagine the scene:

Scurrier Kurt is feeling vaguely uneasy as he phones Dawdler Dan and asks him to come up to his office in the 14th floor executive suite. Kurt hurriedly overcomes the choking feeling in his throat, however, and projects forcefully into the phone, "Hey, Dan, how about coming up to my office right away. I've got a job for you."

Upon receiving the call, Dan begins to get knots in his stomach and chest. He sits quietly at his desk for several minutes pondering why he feels so tense. He begins to reflect on the differences between his and Kurt's ways of doing things. He knows Kurt to be somewhat demanding and intolerant of down time on the job. Yet Dan's own work style generally involves several hours of what he calls, "intuitive reflection" on a problem before he can fully dig into it. "Kurt is more of an *act now, think later* type," Dan muses to himself.

Waiting for Dan to arrive, Kurt makes three or four phone calls, orders a cup of coffee, and is in the middle of composing a letter on his Dictaphone when Dan enters.

"What took you so long!?" Kurt challenges, predictably.

"Uh...I had to get a few things together before I left my desk," Dan defends himself.

The struggle is off to a good start. Each coming at the other from opposite corners, moving with his characteristic moves, playing his assigned role.

The outcome, too, can be foretold. Scurrier Kurt will continue to feel righteous and somewhat frustrated with

Dawdler Dan's unconventional rhythm. Dan will continue to
feel one-down, misunderstood and resentful. The job will get
done, nearly on time, thanks to an eleventh-hour burst of
effort. But the price paid in terms of wasted human energy,
miscommunication and simple joylessness, is totally
unnecessary. Work relationships do not need to be only
tolerable. They can be truly supportive and enlivening if both
parties see this as a possible and worthy aim. The world of
work is so full of such subtle, energy-draining power
struggles that we may tend to see this as just part of the
game. But this need not be so.

Either Dan or Kurt could have made the first move
toward turning the power struggle into dialogue. Kurt, for
example, could have broken the ice with, "I'm trusting you
with an important piece of work, Dan," and continue with
some self-disclosure like, "As you know, I'm the kind of guy
who gets nervous when things aren't in motion all the
time...Your style is different from mine, we both know that.
And I'll admit I'm not altogether comfortable with it, but I
think that's because it *is* so different from mine.... Just tell
me one thing, Dan. What are you doing when I see you at your
desk just looking off into space? I'm not jumping to
conclusions that you're goofing off. It's something I really
need to understand. It's so sort of foreign to me."

Or Dan could have started the conversation on a more
positive, less defensive note, "I want to do a good job for you
and for the team, Kurt. But there's something I'd like you to
know about the way I work...," and so on.

That subtle yet familiar attack-defend communication
pattern can be transformed. Even if only one player decides to
change the rules of the game, that is often all that is
necessary. In work settings, where cooperation is absolutely
essential, both for getting the job done and for maintaining a
positive mental attitude, no one really wants a power
struggle. Many people are relieved if someone else takes the
initiative to establish dialogue and openness. Often people
are simply waiting for permission to operate from the

cooperative instead of the competitive part of themselves.

As a consultant to business and human service organizations for 16 years, I can affirm that even in today's organizations where the hard-driving, competitive style seems to prevail, most workers either explicitly dislike this ethic or at least feel vaguely uncomfortable with it. Power struggles are not a natural part of the world of work. Scurriers and Dawdlers can work side by side in ways that enlarge rather than constrict the range of each. If Scurrier Kurt could see some value in Dawdler Dan's approach to his work, he might become more open to discovering his own capacities for intuitive reflection. While he may not be entirely comfortable with such "dawdling" at first, in time he may discover that instead of diminishing his capacity to stay focused on his goal, a little dawdling now and then brings a new sense of relaxation and confidence to his workstyle. Thus, when a Scurrier can accept a Dawdler's workstyle, he may gain access in the process to a formerly hidden or unused part of himself.

While all this is occurring, the Dawdler is now relieved of a considerable amount of pressure. This tends to free her from the need to defend herself against the Scurrier's pressure, thus allowing her to feel her own power more fully. Also, when one is not being pushed to action from the outside, one is more apt to confront oneself, perhaps coming to recognize the need for a little self-push now and then. The static both-in-their-own-corners polarization becomes reconciled, bringing polarity, vitality and variety back into the relationship.

## The Parallel Player and the Face to Face Player

To the Parallel Player, the ideal relationship is one in which partners relate to each other through independent, mutually supportive activities. Partners may each do separate things and report back to each other at a later time; or they may focus their energies on different aspects of a mutually agreed-upon activity. It is as if they are positioned in parallel, side by side rather than facing one another, in relation to something other than each other — their children, their work, their hobbies or whatever activity they happen to be engaged in.

The Face to Face Player's ideal relationship is based on closely shared activities and experiences. They prefer activity undertaken together rather than independently. Face to Face Players place a premium on time spent in one another's presence, in actual interchange, dialogue or interdependent activity. In the Face to Face relationship, we often find partners positioned facing one another, engaged in some kind of intimate personal exchange. They prefer the sharing of feelings, touches, thoughts, favorite places, plans for their future and sweet intimacies.

When a Parallel Player teams up with a Face to Face Player, conflict is almost inevitable. The Parallel Player wants space, room to move, freedom. The Face to Face Player wants time, togetherness, closeness. In this important and commonly encountered polarity, partners tend to attach certain stereotypical meanings to the other's behavior. The Parallel Player often complains of feeling crowded, smothered, or closely watched. The Face to Face Player feels abandoned, excluded or ignored.

While some people do naturally tend to play one role more than the other, a particular relationship can bring out one side or the other of the same person, depending upon where the other is in terms of preference for togetherness vs. space. For example, Fred, who usually plays the parallel role in his relationships with women, finds himself behaving in an almost clinging-vine way now that he is with Jill, who prefers even more space than he does. In his former marriage to Monica, who seemed to need constant attention, Fred got into the habit of retreating to his study every night after work in order to be alone. With Jill, who spends long hours alone in her studio painting, Fred finds the tables have turned. "Now *I* know what it feels like to need constant attention!" he discloses.

In each one of us there are parallel traits and face to face traits. When I'm with someone who prefers more face to face interchange than I do, I tend to become a bit more of a Parallel Player. When I'm with someone who is more self-contained and introverted, my need for contact is stimulated. This phenomenon is created by my own inner ambivalence regarding how close I wish to be with another. There are two sides to my coin; whatever I seem to be like on the surface, you can be sure that there is an under side to it. As we have already seen, beneath the skin of every Saver there are Spender-like traits; scratch the surface of the Scurrier, and you'll find at least some tendency to dawdle.

Parallel Players, that is those who tend to put their Parallel side out front, are often attracted to Face to Face Players for the same reason Savers are attracted to Spenders and Dawdlers to Scurriers. The other seems to have something that one needs to learn about. One's "under side" is usually a trait that one began to unconsciously suppress at an early age due to feedback from one's environment. If my older sister was a Saver, I became a Spender. If my brother was a Scurrier who hated to waste time and who often became irritated with me for not keeping up with him, I came to see myself as a Dawdler.

The conflict which ensues when Parallel meets with Face to Face is simply a mirror of the inner conflict which occurs when one begins to face an aspect of oneself which has been unconscious. At first this aspect of oneself may seem threatening, since it is often associated with some early childhood situation in which one was ignored or harshly treated. It is common to become hypersensitive or hypercritical when this trait is encountered in others. In time, however, if one stays engaged in the relationship, one may become more relaxed with this quality, both in the other and in oneself.

A partner, in love or in work, can become an effective mirror for one's own unconscious, and an ally on the journey to wholeness, rather than an adversary. If my partner's parallel-style introversion stimulates me to feel nervous, this is a clue that I need to develop a more harmonious relationship with the introvert within myself. Have I perhaps denied full expression of this aspect due to a one-sided self-image adopted at an early age? And can I come to respect this part of myself by learning to respect it in another?

This is how the attraction, polarization, reconciliation process works. I am first attracted to the Parallel Player for his self-containment, his ability to be centered within himself. After a time, this very trait becomes a source of irritation to me. I begin to see his centeredness as imperviousness, his self-containment as withdrawal, as I begin to feel the discomfort arising within myself regarding my own inhibited Parallel Player.

If I, as a Parallel Player, habitually suppress or deny my need for contact, it may continue to grow, eventually exerting force toward expression or recognition. As a result, I may become emotionally reactive when I encounter this trait in others. Whenever we deny recognition to a part of ourselves, we create an unmet need within us which may show itself in increased sensitivity to that characteristic in others. Thus, the Parallel Player may find it quite irritating to be around people who seem to need constant attention. The more deeply she has buried her Face to Face impulses, the more exaggerated, confused and inappropriate are her negative reactions to her opposite. When a Parallel Player acknowledges her own need for close contact with people, she no longer reacts negatively to this trait in others.

Let me summarize by saying that within each of us, there is the need for attention and the need for aloneness. When these needs are in balance, and conscious, that person has perspective on her varying moods. She realizes that sometimes she wants human contact and other times she prefers to withdraw from contact. When one or the other of these needs are unmet, her psyche will be out of balance. She will tend to attract her other pole to her as a natural way of restoring balance.

The attraction-polarization-reconciliation process involves making peace with some unaccepted aspect of oneself by learning to respect it first in another. The process involves projecting onto another some quality which one has not yet become comfortable expressing or acknowledging. Such projection may have a romantic quality, or it may be a source of friction. With continued interaction, one is led to reclaim the projected quality, to accept within oneself the potential for the very same quality. Reclaiming such a projection is the key to reconciliation; I now acknowledge we can *both* be that way!

## The Lover and the Warrior

Some of my women friends and I, when we get together and talk about men, have come to classify men as either Lovers or Warriors.

Lovers are the kind of men who enjoy hanging out, who are never too busy or too tired to enjoy leisurely, non-goal-oriented lovemaking, no matter what the time of day or night. Lovers are often artists, musicians or craftspeople. Usually, they do not hold a regular job and are uncomfortable with schedules.

Warriors are the men who are involved in making their mark on the world. They tend to be ambitious and success-oriented, and thus feel uncomfortable spending too much time and energy in non-goal-oriented pursuits.

The Lovers often attract and are attracted to Warrior women, women who have an independent sense of purpose and a high need for achievement. The Warriors often attract and are attracted to Lover women, women who tend to lean on men for their sense of direction and who are most comfortable in non-achievement-oriented pastimes.

Thus the Lover-Warrior typology is not relevant only to men. Both male and female Lovers are concerned more with how it feels between two people rather than how much either or both accomplishes. Male and female Warriors place a high value on achievement, on making an idea or a plan become a reality. Lovers of both sexes tend to fear being seen as sex objects, while both male and female Warriors tend to fear being used as success objects.

As noted above in the discussions of other polar dimensions, every man and woman has within both a Lover aspect and a Warrior aspect, although one aspect will be more conscious and thus more apparent than the other.

Lovers need to develop the power of their own will. Warriors need to learn about surrender to the will of another. When a Lover teams up with a Warrior, in either love or work, the type of misunderstandings which often arise center around the question, "What factors in our situation do we attempt to influence, and what forces should we simply yield to, allowing them to influence us?"

In a business setting, the Warrior attempts to create and manipulate markets, while the Lover is more likely to shift policy in accordance with market trends. Warriors like a good fight, seeing it as an opportunity to test their power or will. Lovers will often do anything to avoid a fight, preferring to enhance their self-esteem in other ways, e.g., by developing deep empathy and rapport with another.

The power struggles that beset Lovers and Warriors often appear similar to those experienced by Parallel and Face to Face Players. And in fact, sometimes Warriors do tend to behave more like Parallel Players and Lovers like Face to Face Players — but not necessarily. The essence of the Lover-Warrior struggle is a basic difference in their assumptions about how the world works: Lovers tending to feel that the important things in life are controlled by destiny or forces beyond the individual's control; Warriors favoring the notion that one is captain of one's own fate and destiny.

Each side of a partnership, just like each aspect of a person, has a piece of the truth. Together, in balanced proportion, we find the fuller, truer picture. Power struggles occur when one side feels threatened by the opposite characteristic, whether within or in the other person.

David and Kate, a couple in midlife, found themselves in

a classic Lover-Warrior battle when David began to feel
stirring within him a sense of mission about his life. Kate, who
felt no such inner drive, saw David's new-found sense of
mission as "mission-ary-like."

"He's trying to save the world when he can't even find
peace in his own heart," she would criticize. But in David's
experience, "I feel as if I'm being called to live a more public
life, to testify before others about what life has taught me by
creating my own television show."

Kate could not understand the value of such activity. She
felt that the path to a meaningful life was through *being,* not
*doing.* "I see so much misguided, fame-oriented activity
going on all the time...the world is none the better for it....
Why don't people just learn to live in love and simplicity?
Then we wouldn't need people to rush about 'saving the
world'!"

Anyone who has ever felt a sense of calling or vocation
can understand David's Warrior stance. And anyone who has
ever seen the full extent of one's own and others' misguided
actions will understand Kate's caution.

As observers of David and Kate's struggle, we can see
validity in both positions. David's stand reminds us that each
person has a share in what happens to the world we live in.
Thus, it is our place to take action according to our values.
Kate's response reminds us that there is much that goes on in
the world that is beyond our control and comprehension.
Thus, it is our place to try to be receptive to what goes on
around us.

If David and Kate could step outside their polarized
struggle and see that their differences represent two ends of a
polar continuum, they might be able to see that both their
positions are partially valid, and they are complementary.
Perhaps they might then be able to learn from each other. If
Kate, the Lover, could develop empathy for her own inner
Warrior, not only would she and David get along better, she
might also be able to direct her Lover qualities more
intentionally, thus helping David and other Warriors to see
that *being* can be for a purpose.

The world today needs a fuller comprehension of both
Lover and Warrior qualities. There is a need for more people
who can behave as if *we are responsible for what goes on
here*. And these people's actions need to be better informed
than they are about *what is going on here*. If David the
Warrior can develop empathy for his inner Lover, not only will
he have enhanced his ability to move mountains, but more
importantly, he may now be able to sense which mountains
are ready to move!

## The Space Taker and the Space Maker

Some people have very clearly defined preferences,
values, and goals. They tend to initiate activities and provide
direction to others. These people I call Space Takers. They
move into and fill the space around them. Other people are
more flexible in their preferences and have less clearly
defined values. They tend to accommodate easily to whatever
situation they find themselves in. I call them Space Makers.
They leave space around them for others to come into and
structure.

Initially, a Space Taker and a Space Maker will get along
very well in a relationship. The Space Taker says what he
wants and the Space Maker accommodates. Space Takers
need people around them who can follow the direction they
provide. Space Makers need others to provide structure and
direction to their lives.

The Space Taker-Space Maker polarity appears similar to
that of Lovers and Warriors. Space Takers-Space Makers are
mainly concerned with initiating vs. accommodating; in the
Lover-Warrior polarity the key question revolves around
doing vs. being.

In the world of work, a supervisor who is a Space Taker
may get along well with employees who are Space Makers.
However, if part of the supervisor's job is to develop the
employee's leadership potential, then she has to learn to
*make* space so her co-workers can learn to *take* space. This is
often a difficult situation. Space Takers, who feel that they

know how things should be done, may not easily give over control to people who seem uncomfortable taking initiative. For this same reason Space Takers sometimes have difficulty delegating work to Space Makers. But on the whole these two types can work together quite well if they are able to appreciate and accept the differences in their styles.

Henry Winer is one supervisor I know who has a very skillful way of helping his employees and co-workers understand his Space Taking style. Every other month, Henry takes part of a team meeting to have team members speak in turn about their styles of doing things. Henry, as the team leader, starts by letting people know very clearly how he likes to do things and how he hopes people will respond to him. Henry offers this explicit opener as a ''given,'' one of the conditions of this particular workplace. Once Henry has taken his space, he asks others to share how they feel his style might affect their working relationship with him.

In my observation of Henry's meetings, I have noted that he gives everyone on the team a chance to see that ''Henry is not just treating *me* this way... He *is* that way and if I don't like it, at least I know he's that way with everyone. I don't need to take it personally.'' The meetings also give team members a chance to see how other people respond to Henry's rather directive management style. This helps them to see that they are not alone, and, more importantly, to see or offer models for other ways of responding to Henry that they may not have thought about.

The principle that Henry is using by having these team meetings is straightforward: often it is more important that one's way be *respected, heard and validated* than it is to actually *get* one's own way on substantive issues.

In the world of work, as in the domain of love, people want to feel respected and valued. And one very important way to help people feel valued is to listen to them. When I offer my undivided attention to someone and make an effort to probe and understand how it feels to be that person, *that* communicates caring. When a confirmed Space Taker like

Henry Winer can make enough space around himself to allow others to express their feelings, this paradoxically creates all the more space for Henry to do things his way. What's more, now he is doing so with the support and counsel of his co-workers. Rather than allowing them to feel cut off, isolated or misunderstood, he creates conditions for helping them know how to approach him. This gives them the initiative, which, in turn, tends to bring out the Space Maker aspect of Henry, since it puts him in a position that demands that he make room for their approaches.

## The Leaper and the Looker

A Leaper is a person who lives always a little far out on a limb. A Looker always makes sure there's ample support under the limb before venturing out on it. Both Leapers and Lookers will embrace new experiences, but Leapers will do so without much prior research into what may occur when going into the unknown. Thus, the Leaper would just as soon not try to know or predict what lies ahead; the Looker definitely prefers to look and look again before leaping.

Often the Leaper, when paired with a Looker, will feel that the Looker is holding her back. Often the Looker will criticize the Leaper for her restlessness, for the inability to just enjoy comfort and security.

Leapers thrive on newness, variety, discovery, uncertainty, and unpredictability. Lookers thrive just as much on familiarity, comfort, security, certainty, and a sense of control over the environment. Leapers are often more interested in possibilities than in actualities. Lookers want to see the data, the proof, the results.

In my travels as a relationship consultant, I receive many questions from people who see themselves as Leapers being held back by their Looker counterparts. "How can I live my life to the fullest," they ask, "when it seems to threaten my partner so much? Can there be a happy, vital relationship between someone like me and someone like that?"

The answer has two parts: first, consider that, whatever

the struggle between you and another person, it can be seen as a mirror of a conflict occurring within yourself. Within you lives both the need for risk and the need for caution. Perhaps your inner Looker is mistrustful of your tendency to leap before you look. Often just entertaining this idea causes an opening and a softening toward the other person, and to the still-to-be-discovered Looker part of yourself.

The second part of the answer asks the Leaper to recall a relationship with someone who was even more of a risk-taker, whether friend, lover or co-worker. In that situation, did the Leaper prefer to be on "this side" or "the other side" (that is, the more cautious side) of the Looker-Leaper polarity? Leapers usually realize at once that it is more fun to be the adventuresome risk-taker than the stick-in-the-mud.

There's a story that sometimes helps clarify this point. A man who left his wife because she was so cautious and fearful chose for his next mate a woman quite the opposite in type. His new wife was not only an ace sky diver and mountain climber, she also played the stock market and gambled on horses regularly. As if that were not enough, she was eager to try all the new mind-expanding workshops that came along, as well as the new mind-expanding drugs. He was going to make sure he had a woman who could keep up with him. So, guess who's threatened, fearful and cautious in *this* marriage!?

Often, we choose our mates because their particular qualities — even their hang-ups — make it possible for us to feel a certain way or maintain a certain self-image. When the relationship is seen from this expanded perspective, it becomes impossible to blame the partner for one's discomfort.

Again, the key is to stop blaming the other and begin to take responsibility for one's own feelings. The polarization may then move toward reconciliation, and we can feel real appreciation for each other in place of the mysterious attraction that first drew us together.

## The Thinker and the Feeler

Some people base their actions and decisions on analysis of facts and rational logic. Others place more weight on "gut feelings" and intuition. Thinkers are not devoid of feeling, nor are Feelers unable to think. The two types simply differ in the importance given to each of these processes in their lives. Thinkers trust their mental processes more than their gut reactions. They find the world of feelings less familiar and therefore less reliable. Feelers trust their guts and hearts more than their heads. They resist being pinned down to facts or logic as the basis for their actions.

A key difference between the Thinker and the Feeler is in the way the two types process information. Thinkers tend to deal methodically with discrete bits of information, each bit being analyzed separately and sequentially. Feelers tend to deal with information more as a whole rather than in bits. They draw their conclusions from the total gestalt of a situation, often coming to their answers in an instantaneous "aha" experience.

Thinkers strive to appear conscious and aware of what they are doing and why. Feelers prefer to present themselves as compassionate, understanding and insightful.

Feelers and Thinkers are often attracted to one another in a way similar to those of the Savers and Spenders and the Scurriers and Dawdlers we have already met. Each seems to possess a quality that the other needs to better understand.

The power struggles that occur when a Thinker pairs up with a Feeler are usually about whether to place more value on the domain of ideas or the domain of feelings. Thinkers often like to spend time exchanging ideas and concepts. Feelers often prefer talking about their own and other people's feelings, or not talking very much at all.

Another frequent area of conflict between these two is in the making of joint decisions. When a Thinker and a Feeler have to jointly decide on the purchase of a house, for example, how does such a decision occur? The Thinker will make a list of pros and cons for each house being considered, which the

Feeler will look at and then promptly ignore as he challenges the Thinker, "Yes, but which one do you like better? Which one will make us happier?" The Thinker will assure him that the list she has just made is the basis for her likes and dislikes, that her likes are based on what makes sense, on what has more items in its favor than against it. The Feeler will contend that the list is an unnecessary step. "And besides," he may add, "I'd probably only lose the list if I made one."

And so it goes. The Thinker gathers data about decisions from the domain of concepts and logic. The Feeler gathers data from the domain of emotions and preferences. The Thinker keeps trying to teach the Feeler how to think more precisely. The Feeler attempts to show the Thinker the widsom of the heart.

A contemporary sage has advised, "You must learn to think with your heart and feel with your head." This axiom represents the path that the Thinker-Feeler pair is destined to travel if they stay together for any length of time. If good will can be maintained in spite of their differences in style, then some of the partner's character is likely to rub off.

One reason that it is easier for Thinker-Feeler pairs to keep an attitude of good will in their relationship is because this is an area of difference which most people have already heard quite a bit about. Magazines, television,and pop psychology have all given enough attention to this dichotomy, including the addition of such stereotypes as "logical" males and "emotional" females, as to make this difference seem normal.

Actually, any polar difference that one encounters is normal and natural. Polarity is the way of nature. Those who can maintain enough perspective to hold this fact in mind are well-prepared to deal with any differences they may encounter between themselves and others. The behavior of every human alive varies from moment to moment depending upon the situations and which aspects of the personality need expression. One's personal pendulum may swing from pole to pole many times during the span of even one day — from tight-fisted to generous, from rushing to relaxing, from giving orders to asking for help.

In a close love or work relationship, we often become stuck at one or the other end of the pendulum's swing. Polarization of our positions is the result, another product of either-or thinking. When one person over-identifies with or gets stuck at one end of the continuum — as a Saver or a Spender, for example — the other person may over-identify with the opposite pole. Reconciliation occurs when partners can step back far enough to see from a both-and perspective, recognizing that the two opposing poles are actually complementary parts of a whole — and that each side needs the other for balance and completion.

# six: How and Why We Get Stuck in Struggle

I once had a friend who was in love with his car
— a sleek, cream-colored Austin Healey roadster. He almost
never went anywhere without it. He hated to leave it parked
on the street because he was always afraid something might
happen to it. If we went out together to a movie, he would get
up several times during the show, "to go to the men's room."
But I knew he was going out to see how his roadster was
doing. He never parked the car in parking lots, lest other
drivers park too close and chip the paint off his door as they
opened theirs.

One winter evening, coming home from a ride in the
country, we got caught in a snow storm. Visibility was poor,
and the driving was treacherous. Although my friend drove
very carefully, the road was covered with ice under snow, and
we soon skidded off the road into a snowbank. We got out and
surveyed our situation as best we could in the dim yellow light
provided by the barely functional flashlight he had in his
glove compartment. For a long time we stood in the falling
snow just trying to comprehend our situation.

Finally, I raised the issue of whether we could get
ourselves out of the snowbank or we should go for help.
During this discussion it became clear to me that he would

never leave his car to seek help. He just couldn't leave her alone. It also became clear, as we talked it over, that he was unwilling to rock the car back and forth, shifting quickly from forward to reverse in hopes of creating the momentum to lift us over the snow pile. He didn't want to take the chance of damaging the underside of the rather low-slung vehicle. So there we were, stuck in what by this time had become a full-blown blizzard, on a near-zero January evening in Vermont. For comic relief, I suggested we wait a few months for the snow to melt. That seemed to be the only option he considered safe enough. He was so attached to keeping his car in perfect condition that he would endure almost any amount of personal suffering rather than risk damage to his beloved roadster.

Being stuck in the snow with a beautiful, expensive car in which you've invested your life's savings is a little like being stuck in a power struggle. You hate to turn your back on something which represents such an investment of time and energy. You fear doing anything that might involve radical change; and you secretly feel that nothing can really help you anyway.

And so it is with many of us who have spent years developing our personal habits and relationship patterns. They have become like old friends; burdensome friends to be sure, but old and familiar, and we know what to expect of them. It is easier for me to withdraw into hurt feelings — as I have always reacted in the past when my partner speaks to me impatiently — than to do anything new or different to break the cycle. It is easier to continue with what is comfortable and familiar than to perhaps respond with humor or with a direct statement of what I am feeling. Perhaps, if I maintain my attitude of hurt feelings, I can convince him of how wrong he is for mistreating me; or so I tell myself. It seems I will tell myself almost anything in order to justify maintaining my familiar ways of coping.

Sometimes I fear that, if I were to change, I might not even feel like myself anymore. I would have to learn new ways of thinking and behaving. Others might come to regard me in new and different ways.

## Four Ways to Stay Stuck in Struggle

In my work with couples and business organizations I've identified four common ideas that fuel power struggles. Each of these notions — all very human — involves some form of fearfulness and some degree of attachment to an unchanging point of view. As I describe them and how they affect relationships, I will also illustrate how each pattern can be successfully changed.

Here's my list of attitudes and feelings guaranteed to keep you struggling:
— Fear of the Past Repeating Itself
— Fear of the Future Turning Out Wrong
— Attachment to Having Your Way
— Expecting the World to be as You Wish It Were

## Fear of the Past Repeating Itself

Generally, whenever a person is hurt, threatened or disappointed, the organism's biologically-based survival mechanism is activated, both physically and psychologically. Physically, the back goes up, the head hunches down into the shoulders, and the area around the heart tenses up to protect the soft and vulnerable parts. Psychologically, a similar process occurs. Often an unconscious "decision" is made right then and there: "I'm not going to let this happen to me ever again!"

In order to uphold this decision to protect yourself from the possible recurrence of such pain, you arm yourself with certain defensive attitudes — again, both physical and psychological. Such attitudes may be designed to prevent you from ever again being exposed to such a potentially hurtful situation. Or your attitude may simply act to numb your sensitivity to pain so that even if such an event should recur, next time you won't *feel* it.

The sort of attitude that prevents one from ever getting into such a situation again is shown by the person who, after a painful marriage breakup, never "bothers" to get a divorce. That way he'll never have to worry about another failed marriage... Or the person who, after being fired from a job, finds herself unable to look for another... Or the person who develops a pattern of "love 'em and leave 'em" after being abandoned by a first true love, so as to always leave lovers before they have the chance to leave.

An example of the second attitude, numbing oneself emotionally so as not to feel pain, is shown by the person who, after a disappointing love affair, now goes into relationships "prepared" to be rejected: "I don't really expect him to love me as much as I love him. Men are all so preoccupied with their careers. But, I don't mind..." Or the person who loses a big promotion to a junior co-worker and says, "I knew that was going to happen; I've taken a lot of hard knocks in my time. Better me than him — he would've been devastated."

These ways of preventing the past from repeating itself also prevent you from learning any other way of coping with such a situation. If you never try again, you never have a chance to learn from your experience. This tends to reinforce your fear of the past. We fear what we do not know how to deal with or what we do not understand.

*Sally Monroe's Four-Year Marriage: A Case Example* — Sally Monroe was an attractive 43-year old woman with the buoyancy and vitality of a 17-year old. Despite many years of experience as a homemaker and professional financial consultant, she exuded an almost naive freshness.

After Sally's third marriage ended in divorce, however, she began to question more deeply the way she was living her life. She decided to go to a counselor in an effort to understand why each of her three marriages had lasted only four years. As she responded to her counselor's questions, she saw that there had been no overt crises that caused the breakups. Instead, Sally simply seemed to lose interest in the marriage right after the start of its fourth year, *in all three cases*. She had left behind three bewildered ex-husbands, all of whom she still loved. She just couldn't stay with anyone beyond the fourth year.

Overt power struggles began in all of Sally's relationships toward the middle of the third year of marriage. This was when she reported that she began to feel "itchy." Her husbands apparently sensed this and responded with demands for increased proof of loyalty and commitment. This tended to make Sally feel closed in, leading her to spend more and more time alone or away from her partner. Thus, with each of her husbands, Sally found herself in a sort of tug-o-war in which she felt captive in a relationship which no longer carried any meaning for her.

After several months of counseling, Sally and her counselor were probing into hurtful or disappointing experiences from Sally's childhood. As they searched Sally's memory for significant incidents, Sally suddenly broke into tears, crying out in a little-girl voice, "Daddy, don't leave me. I don't want you to go!" She repeated this phrase over and over for the next several minutes.

When Sally finally was ready to let her sobbing subside, she had a clear, refreshed look on her face. Sitting up very straight and smiling at her counselor, she confided, "That happened when I was four years old. The United States had just entered the second World War. My father had to go into the Army at that time, and my mother and I took him to the train station. It wasn't until he was about to get on the train that I realized what was happening, that he was leaving for good, or at least for a very long time. I sensed the pain of separation that both my parents were feeling, and that clued me in to the seriousness of the situation. I was feeling their pain as well as my own. And I was determined to get my daddy to stay. But he left. I had no influence in the situation. I felt so helpless, so powerless. I was crushed. It was then that I remember thinking to myself, 'They always leave just when you want them to stay... I can't let this ever happen again. I'll make sure it won't!' And I must've decided that it takes about four years of things being good for that kind of thing to happen... Yes, that's it! I know something in me changed on that day.''

Sally Monroe's insight into her four-year relationship pattern allowed her to make a conscious *adult* decision to risk "being left again at the train station." The last I heard about Sally, she had remarried once again and was just entering her *tenth* year of marriage, having experienced no urge to leave the relationship.

*Getting Through the Fear* — To move through a fear of the past repeating itself it is first necessary to recognize what you have been doing, as Sally did. Acknowledging that it is *your* fear and yours to deal with is the beginning of taking responsibility for the pattern. You may need to watch your pattern in operation over time, noticing which instances trigger the fear and what your automatic reaction is. This observation period helps you understand the function the pattern serves in your life, what it helps you to attain or to avoid, including any secondary gains, such as the opportunity for self-pity. Letting go of the pattern will probably mean sacrificing these payoffs.

Sometimes, however, such an observation period is not necessary. It is possible to experience a breakthrough in awareness in an instant, similar to Sally's sudden insight after several months of counseling. Such awareness may produce profound changes in one's inner being — a new feeling of *wholeness* perhaps. When one becomes aware of an inner part that has been hidden — such as Sally's little-girl-who-feared-abandonment — the unconscious influence of this part is reduced. And that formerly hidden part of the personality may begin an active inner relationship with other parts. Thus, Sally's wish for continuity in relationships was reconciled with her fear of being abandoned.

Once formerly unconscious fears become accepted, they can be dealt with consciously. Instead of dominating, they become only a part of the total decision-making process. You can allow yourself to *feel* your fears, but still go ahead and *do* whatever it is you're choosing to do (such as stay in a relationship even though you fear the pain of being left). When you discover the source of your fears, and begin to understand them, they no longer exert so much power and control in your life.

## Fear of the Future Turning Out Wrong

Fritz Perls, originator of Gestalt Therapy, summarized a great deal in his little phrase, ''Anxiety is the gap between now and the future.'' People who live with an eye always on the future can become so concerned that the future may not turn out well that they seem unable to do much of anything. Doing nothing helps them avoid anxiety about mistakes, but it costs them their vitality.

If you have great difficulty making decisions, perhaps you are one of those who needs to know how things will turn out before you attempt something new. This can get pretty boring after a while. It can also lead to frequent struggles with those around you who may wish to be in a growing relationship with you, since it tends to leave you unable to make a commitment.

But what if you *are* uncomfortable and anxious about acting without sufficient information or leaping into the unknown? What can be done? Is it possible to understand yourself well enough to change a deep-seated pattern? Certainly rational arguments about how you ''should'' behave don't help.

It can help to realize that your whole personality is being dominated by a single aspect. You have other aspects, of course, but they may not find expression until you come to a new understanding of the part of you that fears making a mistake. Such understanding may require sincere and concentrated self-study, or even intensive psychotherapy.

Your self-examination must address a wide range of questions: Where did this fear come from? How old were you when it first began to dominate your personality? Who, if anyone, in your early life seemed to feel similarly about making mistakes? What does this part of you fear may happen if things don't turn out well? Has anything like the feared event ever actually *happened* to you?

These sorts of questions can lead you to see and accept this part of yourself for the function it serves in your overall ''emotional economy.'' Perhaps the part once had a useful function in your life which is now outdated. Perhaps it can still have a useful moderating effect but needs to be viewed in relationship to the aspects of your personality which seek learning, variety and discovery. Your caution about the future can be useful, as long as it is not allowed to dominate your decisions.

*The Case of Miss Goodie Two Shoes* — Patricia Clay was a single woman in her early 30's who couldn't seem to attract the kind of man she dreamed of as a mate. In every man she met, she could see the potential problems in the relationship. With each new lover, she tended to focus on what could lead to pain and disappointment in the future, rather than on his positive qualities which she could enjoy now. As a result she found herself constantly struggling, both within herself and with her partners, over the question of whether to put her energy into the relationship or to withdraw her interest and look elsewhere for a suitable companion. Whenever a man became really interested in her, she would seem to sabotage the relationship by constantly talking about what might go wrong between them: ''Maybe we won't be able to have children... Maybe we'll have more children than we can afford... Maybe you'll lose your job... Maybe you'll become so engrossed in your work that you won't have time for me....'' Patricia could go on like that for hours!

In searching to understand the roots of this pattern, Patricia began seriously to observe her feelings, reactions, and motives. Focusing her search on the self-examination questions listed above, she discovered what she felt to be the genesis of the pattern. When she was a young girl of about 10, her alcoholic parents had done many irresponsible and embarrassing things in Patricia's presence. An only child, Patricia felt it was up to her to maintain some semblance of order in the household and propriety vis-a-vis outsiders.

Since she found she could not control her parents or get them to behave properly, Patricia began to over-control herself. She wore clothes that were always neat, crisp and clean. She never used slang or obscenities. She conformed completely to all school and church rules. And she never did anything which did not have a completely predictable outcome. If she was ever called on unexpectedly in school, she became tongue-tied, unable to risk giving a wrong answer. Yet this rarely happened to Patricia, since she usually overprepared her school assignments.

She recognized this early pattern as an attempt to maintain a sense of control in her life — to keep from being overwhelmed by her parents' frequent unpredictable and chaotic emotional outbursts. "I became 'Miss Goodie Two Shoes'," she disclosed, "in order to cover up how bad and guilty I felt for having parents like that.... I couldn't *stand* to do anything wrong. My whole self-esteem was built upon being different from my parents."

She soon began to understand other influences from her early years: "My father actually had a part in him just like me. 'Don't ever do anything unless you can be the very best at it,' he used to say. He was so dominated by this part that the only time he could get away from it was when he was loaded. So I guess I was unconsciously living out this part of my father, since he couldn't live it for himself. He never had much fun... he was always so worried about things turning out wrong... unless he was drunk."

Patricia saw that she had developed an obsessive concern for controlling the future during a time when much of her world was in chaos. She saw how she had imitated many of her father's attitudes while at the same time striving to be different from her parents. She saw that her anxiety was not so much about the future, but rather a fear of her own inadequacy and powerlessness. And most importantly, she saw that this pattern was no longer needed in her life. In her present life, she was in no danger of being overtaken by chaos. On the contrary, she was in danger of being overtaken by order! And she already had the respect and admiration of many other people, which was something she'd been trying to achieve via her role as "Miss Goody Two Shoes." What Patricia needed was to share the love of another person, in spite of the uncertainties involved.

As with most of us, it was not easy for her to move from these insights to a change in behavior. She had been allowing her fears to block her ability to act for many years. This had led her to feel less and less potent and influential in her life, thus increasing her fear that her actions would be ineffectual or lead to undesireable consequences. Patricia had to learn to act, to decide, just as if she were a baby learning to take its first steps. She did this by starting with small inconsequential decisions, "baby steps" into the unknown. Gradually, with the help of an understanding partner, she took bigger steps toward the unknown future.

As she was able to live in the present more fully, she came to feel more powerful and more confident about the actions she was taking. This brought her to the point where she became more willing to let the future be as it would be, to trust the unknown. As she let go of her worries about the future, she had more of her attention available to see and cope with the realities of the present. A behavior change which had once seemed impossible now became self-reinforcing: the more she used her attention for dealing with the present, the less anxiety she felt about the future.

Patricia's story recalls a general principle which applies to fears of the future: *as the present becomes more knowable and more known to us, our anxiety lessens, and we are able to let the future take care of itself.*

## Attachment to Having Your Way

Have you ever noticed how people who try to get their way all the time are almost always frustrated and angry people? These are the people who are so important to themselves that they have little capacity for being concerned with anyone else's well-being. Yet because they are so overly focused on helping themselves, others tend to be less interested in helping them. They appear to be taking care of number one, so why should anyone else look out for their interests? Thus, they often feel as if no one cares and sometimes even as if the world is against them.

Before we start blaming or judging these people, let's consider why they are the way they are. Why do they seem so focused on having their own way to the exclusion of consideration for others?

People often treat others the way they were treated in early life. Thus, a person who never *received* recognition and attention as a youngster will have difficulty *giving* recognition and attention. Someone who was never listened to as a child will have trouble listening to others. If you were left to fend for yourself during the formative years, you will likely expect others to take care of themselves.

People who seek to get their own way are simply following the examples of their early models and teachers. One cannot usually offer to others what one has never received. Our early family experiences are our schooling in interpersonal relationships. Unfortunately, in many families the parents haven't had the good fortune themselves of having learned how to listen or to offer sincere undivided attention. It's a vicious cycle: very few adults were really recognized or listened to as children, so they are ill-prepared to tutor their children in the arts of listening and giving attention to others' needs.

How can this cycle be broken? How can one learn the joys of really listening to others when there are so few people around to demonstrate this ability?

I believe that people who find themselves continually stuck in their own positions are really longing to be recognized, attended to, or cared about. They listen only to themselves because they were never able to depend on others for the recognition they sought. They hang on tightly to their viewpoints, trying to get the fair hearing they have never really had. They are sincerely, though unconsciously, trying to get something that every human being deserves — attention. Being with others who really hear them and care about their needs and views often moves such persons to relax their over-concern about getting their way.

The way out of the pattern of selfishness is to gain the experience of being treated unselfishly. In order to find someone to help you gain this experience, you may need to humbly and openly acknowledge the gap in your learning about how to be with other people. Tell others how you came to be as you are, and ask them for help. This allows them to give you what you need without feeling used or abused, for you are acknowledging their gift to you.

As you become more accepting of your longing to be heard or recognized, your way of expressing this need will become gentler and more open, less embarrassing, less awkward. People will see that you are motivated by your wish for recognition rather than by a wish to dominate or overpower. Most hard, callous behavior is a cover-up for softer, more vulnerable feelings. And when you are able to show others your needs rather than your demands, they will be more likely to respond to you.

In addition to its disarming effect on others, expressing yourself in a softer way also opens you up to yourself. By acknowledging your longing to be heard, you come to accept yourself in a new way. You give attention to the child part of you which has always longed for such caring attention, and in so doing, you are recognizing and listening to yourself — a necessary ingredient for engaging the attention of others.

To summarize this point, we tend to have trouble receiving from others what we cannot give to ourselves. Yet it is also very difficult to give to ourselves what we have never received from others. Attention and recognition are rather like work experience. The young person seeking a first job is told by many employers to "get some experience." "But how," laments the youngster, "do I get experience when no one will hire me?"

One has to begin somewhere, of course, whether the goal is getting a job or meeting a need for personal recognition. I have suggested that you begin by acknowledging and recognizing the child in you who wishes to be heard. This helps you draw others to you, who can then appreciate and accept you as you are.

## Expecting the World to Be As You Wish It Were

Some people accept life as it is. Others question the way things are and envision higher possibilities. Some of those in this second category seem always to be fighting against the way they find things. "Life shouldn't be like this!" they seem to be protesting, "It should be easier, fairer, more just!"

"Jobs should be more fulfilling and pay higher wages.... Families should be loving, not strife-torn.... Spouses should honor and respect one another.... The world should be different.... I can't accept living this way."

People who expect the world to be as they wish are not usually trying to make things good only for themselves. They often have quite altruistic motives. Yet their attempts to change things are often ineffective because they are based on *expectations* that things should be different. Such an attitude is likely to meet with resistance in the environment, since it comes from a resistant attitude inside the person.

Such resistance to how one finds things — to *what is* — blurs one's perception of current realities. All sorts of surplus or distorted information may be "seen" when one's attention is fixed on what *could* or *should* be instead of on what *is*. Such distortions make it hard to deal adequately with the present reality, and often lead to feelings of powerlessness or inadequacy. People often defend against such feelings by focusing *externally* — on how their expectations have been disappointed — rather than *internally* — on changes needed in themselves: ''I was in line for that promotion. It *should* have gone to me!'' ...''We're married now, so we *should* be having sex regularly.'' By focusing attention on others, one need never confront one's own responsibility in the situation. Unfortunately, this means that the situation will probably never change!

Disappointment is a close relative of anger. Someone to whom you direct your anger will likely become defensive and resistant to you. If you are continually hurt and disappointed by life, it may make others around you feel guilty or irritated in your presence. This may lead them to either avoid being around you or to try to get you to change, another classic setup for a power struggle.

People who have a lot of expectations of how others ''should be'' are often projecting onto others their own unacknowledged personal needs. They expect others to behave in ways that they themselves cannot. But wait a minute! In relationships we tend to attract those qualities we need to learn about. Thus, those with high expectations are likely to keep on attracting others whose qualities they cannot accept. Sooner or later, such persons must come to acknowledge *in themselves* whatever feelings or qualities they have been avoiding.

*Expecting the world to be different than it is* is generally rooted in a lack of self-acceptance, which in turn implies a lack of self-knowledge. Knowing yourself is easier if you adopt a both-and view of yourself. Instead of seeing yourself as either hard-working or carefree, either selfish or unselfish, the more flexible both-and perspective allows you to see yourself as somtimes carefree *and* sometimes hard-working. You are actually both. As you relax your inflexible expectations of yourself, you tend also to relax your expectations of others.

As you come to know yourself, you also come to realize that the way you are and the things that are happening to you make sense, given your particular set of life experiences and lessons to learn. If you were a different person, your world would be different. And one way to become different than you are, and therefore change the world you live in, is to feel different about the events around you.

*It's not what happens to you that makes you happy or unhappy, but how you handle what happens to you.* If you handle things in a way you can respect, then you will accept life. If you handle your life's events in a way that makes you feel contemptible or inadequate, then you will resent life for putting you in such a predicament.

*The Case of the Disappointed President* — Terrance LaFlamme was president of a multi-million dollar computer software corporation, employing over 1,000 people. The Boston-based business had come to him suddenly through the untimely death of his father, a self-made man of towering stature, who had founded the company and built it to its present strength.

Whereas his father's presence in any of the company's five buildings could be heard or felt for hundreds of yards, the unassuming Terrance could walk through the corridors virtually unnoticed. Though Terrance was of medium height, about 5' 10", to most employees he seemed much shorter, since they tended to compare him to his 6' 4" father. But whether the employees were ready to accept Terrance or not, he was their new president. At 38, he seemed young to many of them, even though they did respect his technical expertise.

As for Terrance, he felt quite ready to take over the presidency, at least in terms of his technical knowledge of the business. He was extremely unsure of himself, however, when it came to dealing with people. He was also a very proud man, who found it difficult to admit his uncertainty to others, or even to himself.

As soon as his presidency was announced, Terrance began to focus his concern on how well his managers and vice presidents showed their respect to him. He expected to be treated as a president "should" be treated — more specifically, as his father had been treated. Predictably, since Terrance's relationship to the company and to top management was different from his father's, people were not going to regard him in the same way. By expecting something that simply was not to be, Terrance was setting himself up for disappointment.

His loss, however, was not without secondary gain. Though painful, his disappointment was still not as painful for him as it would have been to feel, and perhaps express, his doubts about his capacity to deal with the employees as people. By focusing on the *failure of others* to meet his expectations, he was able to avoid feeling his softer uncertain-about-himself feelings. In his attempt to cover up his self-doubts, he was prone to react with irritation to the least sign of lack of respect from his co-workers. He became hypercritical of those employees whose loyalty he doubted. This led to frequent disagreements about how a job should be performed — Terrance's way of testing the employee's respect and deference.

As Terrance's tenure as president wore on, more and more of his employees were feeling confused and resentful about his meddling in their domains of work. And Terrance himself was beginning to wonder if being president was worth all the headaches he had inherited.

Were Terrance's headaches a necessary part of his new role? What if he had chosen a different way of dealing with his uncertainties about himself? What if, instead of thinking about how others had disappointed him, he had quietly looked into himself and seen that his blaming others for his discomfort was a way to avoid his self-doubts? What if he had then acknowledged in himself a need for their help in adjusting to his new position? And what if he had then elected to express his wants and needs directly?

We can imagine that people might have been eager to offer Terrance their support if he had been able to say, ''I need...'' instead of ''You should....'' People feel more open and kind toward someone who acknowledges his needs rather than trying to cover up his weaknesses. When you try to cover your weaknesses, you are not being honest with yourself and others. This tends to create muddled and confusing communication, often leading to misunderstanding and needless struggle. When you are open with others about your self-perceived weaknesses, others are more apt to accept you in spite of them.

When you can admit to others your softer feelings, even if you yourself cannot fully accept having such feelings, you may be surprised to find how easily others can accept you. This brings you closer to being able to feel both soft and strong at the same time. You begin to find you are able to accept yourself in spite of what you once called weaknesses, because you now see these frailties as simply a part of your humanness.

# seven: Anatomy of an Argument

**Brenda and Bruce,** both 25, have been married for five years. They have known each other since high school, where he played football and basketball, and where she was a cheerleader and prom queen. All during high school and college, they were known by their friends as the perfect couple. Their relationship was the envy of all their friends. Even their parents and their parents' friends held Bruce and Brenda's relationship up as a model of harmony and togetherness. And, for the first several years of their marriage, Brenda and Bruce were able to live up to these glowing impressions of marital contentment, but after they graduated from college and both went to work, tensions began to arise....

I'll get back to Brenda and Bruce shortly. First, let's take a closer look at what happens in a classic relationship conflict.

Power struggles may be triggered by differences in wants, perceptions, rhythms or styles. Yet struggle is only one possible reaction to such differences.

Another reaction is learning: learning to see the situation with greater perspective; learning to see oneself more completely. For most people, whether a difference leads to struggle or learning depends upon how the conflict is interpreted. It is easy to maintain perspective when the difference offers no threat to the persons or the relationship. It is a lot harder when the difference is potentially destructive to your security or sense of well-being. Later in this chapter, I'll discuss a couple who experienced just such a highly threatening power struggle, involving whether to open their marriage to other sex partners.

When confronting such emotionally volatile differences in wants, how one interprets the difference is of course very important. Even more important is how open the two people can be to trying to understand each other, how willing they are to be moved or influenced by each other's feelings.

In most work relationships, and many love relationships as well, differences frequently arise over how a particular job should be done or how a particular problem should be solved; in other words, a difference in style. Here, again, how the two people interpret their difference is crucial: Is it seen as a challenge to either person's competence or authority, or is it accepted calmly as a matter of course? How open the two are to each other is again a vital determinant of whether or not the difference leads to struggle. An additional ingredient is the degree to which the partners are at peace within themselves.

There are three important things to consider, then, which determine whether a difference will lead to a power struggle:

— how the meaning of the difference is interpreted;

— how open each is to understanding and being influenced by the other;

— how much inner harmony or conflict each is feeling.

In order to illustrate how each of these factors operates to provoke and resolve power struggles, let's examine conflicts in the lives of three real partnerships. First, we'll get back to Bruce and Brenda, our model match....

## ''I'm Not in the Mood, Bruce.''

After college, Brenda took a job as a social worker. She

spends all day in an office full of people, interviewing clients and exchanging clinical opinions with her co-workers. Often her days are full of intense emotional interchange. She finds herself developing strong feelings of warmth and caring for her clients, and she is beginning to develop close friendships with two of the other young women in her office. As a result, she often returns home from work emotionally spent and in need of a quiet undemanding atmosphere.

Bruce, meanwhile, went to work as a research chemist. His days are spent primarily alone, following a brief morning meeting with his supervisor, with whom he has only a formal business-like relationship. All day long Bruce's only interactions are with his microcomputer, "Sophia," and various other laboratory devices. Most people at the lab where he works bring bag lunches, which they eat by themselves as they continue to work. Bruce has adopted this practice also, more as a concession to the norms of the workplace than as a matter of choice. He would like to become friendly with some of his colleagues, but no one seems to have the time.

When they arrive home from work at the same hour each day, the scene is predictable. Brenda needs time to be alone, to putter around the kitchen or with her houseplants. She prefers a period of quiet time before exchanging affection and conversation with Bruce. He, on the other hand, is eager for some contact and togetherness after spending all day alone at the lab.

As objective observers of Brenda and Bruce, it is easy for us to see how the rhythm and pace each has experienced all day at work affects the mood they each bring to their daily time of reunion. But for Brenda and Bruce it is not so easy to be objective. After all, they were the perfect couple. *They* shouldn't be having marital problems. What is happening to them? Why do they feel so uncomfortable together so much of the time?

All Bruce knows is that when he approaches Brenda as she comes into the kitchen from the garage, he feels like

hugging and kissing for a while and then exchanging little
news items from the day's events at work. But when he tries
to put his arms around her, her response has become
painfully predictable: "I'm not in the mood, Bruce. I need a
little time for myself for a while." This leaves Bruce feeling
confused and hurt.

All Brenda can be sure about is that Bruce has become
awfully needy lately and this makes her uncomfortable. She
has an inkling that if he could just give her a little more
breathing room at the end of the working day, later on in the
evening she would feel like talking and being affectionate. It's
just that he seems so intent on satisfying *his* need and so
insensitive to *hers*! This is the meaning she has given to their
difference in rhythm and mood. In expressing his need, she
feels he is ignoring hers.

Bruce, for his part, has also arrived at an interpretation
of their disharmony. He believes that Brenda's need for alone
time reflects her waning interest in him. As a result he has
begun to test her love in little ways. Often, for example, he
will ask her to do something for him, such as to make him a
cup of tea or a sandwich, when he knows she is busy doing
something else. "If she really loved me," he reasons, "she
would be happy to do these little things." Bruce can see that
Brenda gets impatient with him when he tries to engage her
in conversation after they have each returned home from
work, but he doesn't understand her impatience and is afraid
to ask about it. He feels that if she could simply offer him a
little warmth and attention, he would be satisfied; and then
they could both go on about their separate household tasks or
hobbies. He can't imagine that her need at the end of the day
might simply be different from his. Instead, he secretly feels
she is being stubborn and withholding.

She can't accept the difference either. In her mind, she
blames the tension on Bruce's insensitivity to her needs,
never realizing that she too could be accused of insensitivity.

Brenda and Bruce have not forgotten how much they
once loved each other, and they vow to do whatever is

necessary to find that love again. This vow helps them weather their difficulties a bit more easily, but it does not resolve the tension.

In the case of Brenda and Bruce, the resolution comes almost by accident. There is a cut in the city budget which has supported Brenda's position. As a result, she and several of her co-workers are required, because of lack of seniority, to reduce their worktime to a six-hour day instead of the usual eight. With this change in her work schedule, Brenda now arrives home at 3:30 in the afternoon, two hours before Bruce's return. This gives her plenty of time to unwind and relax, perhaps to go jogging or take a nap, before she has to even think about what to have for dinner. Usually, she has dinner well in progress and is beginning to feel time on her hands as Bruce walks into the kitchen, looking for his hug and exchange of news. Now, with her new schedule, Brenda is happy to see Bruce come through the door. She has been alone enough and is ready for some togetherness.

Brenda and Bruce fall easily back into love now that circumstances have assisted them in synchronizing their rhythms.

While differences in rhythm or mood may instigate a power struggle, such differences are not the actual cause of struggle. The root cause often has more to do with how each person views the difference. When Bruce interpreted Brenda's need for time alone as a reflection of a waning interest in him, he began to do little things to test her love, which only added to the tension between them. If he could have seen her behavior as a way to help herself unwind at the end of the workday, instead of as a way of rejecting him, he could probably have felt more relaxed about their differing rhythms. Likewise, if Brenda could have seen Bruce's need for warmth and contact as an acceptable expression of his feelings, she might have dealt with his approaches more casually and with less defensiveness and irritation.

As it occurred, Brenda and Bruce were the beneficiaries of a fortunate accident. Their power struggle was resolved

without either of them coming to any deep insights or
changing in any significant way. Most power struggles are not
so easily resolved, as we shall see in the next two examples.

## The Ambivalent Marriage of Bart and Betty

Bart came home from a business trip, after being married
to Betty for six months, and announced that he now wanted to
include other sex partners in his life. Betty was devastated.
She cried almost non-stop for three days. Bart was
bewildered. He felt that all he had done was to "open the
*subject* — not the marriage!" Betty felt that Bart's new
feelings spelled doom for the relationship. Bart felt it was no
big deal. He loved his wife very much and couldn't
understand her exaggerated reaction.

They sought help from a couples counselor in order to see
if they could come to some agreement on the issue. Each took
a strong position that the marriage couldn't work unless the
other was willing to change: Bart knew that if he let Betty
stand in the way of his sexual self-expression, he would surely
grow to resent her; Betty was certain that she was not willing
to share Bart's sexual attentions with other women, since she
felt far from satisfied with the amount of sexual contact they
were presently having. Their power struggle seemed at an
impasse. What help could counseling offer?

When they came into the counselor's office, they were
acting like the best of friends. Emotions were muffled to
non-existent. Yet it was obvious that each felt disappointed
and misunderstood.

In order to help them get to the root of their
disagreement, the counselor asked to hear first the story of
their relationship, and then the stories of their individual
lives.

As these stories unfolded, it was easy to see how Bart
and Betty had arrived at an impasse.

During courtship, Betty had been attracted to Bart's
worldliness, his power in business and social affairs. He, on
the other hand, had been attracted to her tenderness, her

ability to relax and just "be," and her single-minded devotion to him. The counselor suspected that beneath these overt reasons for initial attraction were other less obvious, growth-oriented motives. Bart wanted to learn from Betty about "being," about relaxation and tenderness. Betty wanted to learn from Bart about "doing," about power and worldliness. Each was attempting to know his or her other side by first coming to know it in the partner.

However, one's other side is usually unconscious — and usually for good reason. Often it is the aspect of oneself that was either ignored or punished during one's infancy or childhood — the part that did not win any points and may even have brought reprisal. This aspect of one's potential then becomes submerged in the shadows of the personality. Yet it may still exert subtle (or unconscious) pressure toward expression. This is why we are often attracted to people who seem so opposite from us.

So, in the beginning, he loved her for her "lovingness" and she loved him for his power. After a time, however, Bart's wordly power began to look to Betty like a "neurotic striving for fame and glory. He's never got time just to hang around the house and *be* together," she complained, "and even if he is at home with me, he's always *doing* at least three things at once!"

For Bart's part, his feelings about Betty's devotion to him also began to change. What once looked like "lovingness" began to feel more like over-dependency and a tendency to smother him.

Betty and Bart were two very disappointed people. Each had thought the other was a dream-come-true partner, but after only six months of marriage, they woke up to find themselves living a nightmare.

The first disappointment in a relationship is often the hardest. It is often also the trigger for crisis, such as the crisis that occurred when Bart announced to Betty his wish to "open" their marriage. Crisis can be a way of calling attention to the back-log of frustration and disappointment in a marriage. It can then be used to uncover buried hurt and angry feelings that have built up over time.

As this uncovering process continued, the counselor also learned that Betty and Bart had never actually discussed their intentions about whether their marriage should include or exclude other sex partners. Each had vaguely assumed that the other knew and accepted what they wanted. Betty knew she wanted an exclusive contract but now admitted that she had been a little afraid of telling this to Bart directly for fear of putting him off. Bart, too, had known from the beginning that he had a roving eye, but he couldn't tell this to Betty for fear of losing her. He told himself that this might be changing (at least it seemed to be during the Romance Stage!), so why create an unnecessary hassle.

It was only after Betty's behavior began to disappoint him that his eye began to rove. He said he felt trapped, and his way of coping with this was to seek the variety of other lovers.

Bart was not the only one whose commitment was affected by disappointment, however. Betty recognized that her sexual openness toward Bart had decreased as her disappointment increased. She still felt she "wanted his company sexually," but she had to admit that she was holding a lot of herself back from him. "It was as if my heart began to grow a protective armor around it. I couldn't respond to him the way I did in the beginning." These subtle inner changes in one partner became obvious to the other and affected the bond between them. Betty felt Bart's disappointment and gradual withdrawal of attention. Bart felt Betty's disappointment and the cooling of her responsiveness.

Undercurrents of this sort are behind all intimate power struggles. The overt issues or causes may vary depending on the personalities of the people involved, but the underlying reasons for this sort of power struggle often involve disappointed expectations.

From here, couples generally go in one of two directions: either they *put more into* the relationship, by communicating their hurt and disappointment; or, more commonly, they *partially withdraw* from the relationship, perhaps seeking compensation through work, hobbies, or outside relationships. Often, at this juncture, one member of the couple will take the former course while the other will take the latter. In the case of Bart and Betty, she sought more attention from Bart, while he wanted to put more of his attention outside their relationship.

As the counseling process unfolded, Bart and Betty were able to look at some of the basic differences in their needs for contact. This difference began to surface on their honeymoon — a two-week vacation on a remote Caribbean island, where there was nothing to do except be together. As they looked back on this period, they saw that they had had very different experiences during that time together. Betty confessed that she had fallen more deeply in love with Bart during that trip. ''He wasn't so distracted with work and phone calls and his computer games as he is when we're at home... For the first time, I felt he really paid attention to *me*... I thought to myself, 'There's hope after all for Bart... Maybe he is able to just *be* sometimes.' ''

Bart's recollections of the trip were quite different: ''I was bored most of the time. There just wasn't enough to *do*... That was when I really started to feel hemmed in. I thought to myself, 'I'm trapped in a marriage that doesn't suit my temperament.' But I decided to try and push those feelings aside and do things Betty's way.''

Obviously Bart's plan to push his trapped feelings aside didn't work. His first extended business trip away from home rekindled his desire for freedom and ''time out'' from the marriage. By that time, Bart was beginning to feel Betty's ''smothering dependency'' instead of the ''single-minded devotion'' to him that had originally been such a strong source of attraction. He acknowledged that he wanted more from life than love and marriage. He wanted to produce really outstanding and socially beneficial films. And Betty's ''hunger for constant attention'' was costing him too much time away from his work.

By this time, Betty had begun to revise her opinion about Bart's worldliness. "He's just another over-achiever, hungry for fame and power," she disclosed to the counselor, "he can't just let things or himself be as they are. He's always tinkering or manipulating things. It's as if he doesn't feel he has a right to be alive if he isn't *working* on something."

As counseling proceeded, the counselor attempted to help Bart and Betty see how their early family histories had contributed to their present situation. Bart had come from a family where he was the younger of two children. He had a sister, three years older than he, who had often looked after him in a rather bossy manner, thus contributing to his feeling of being crowded or trapped when in the close company of a female. His mother had been a sort of strong, all-suffering victim/martyr in relationship to a tyrannical-but-self-doubting alcoholic father. His father would become abusive to both Bart and his mother during his alcoholic binges, mysteriously ignoring or even favoring his sister.

His early family situation left Bart with both a feeling of competitiveness with women (as he'd felt with his sister) and an expectation that women could and would tolerate all manner of abuse from men (as his mother had done). His father's low self-esteem and sense of failure as a breadwinner made Bart determined not to follow in his father's footsteps, yet at the same time left him with a nagging sense of doubt about his own adequacy in the world of work and as a man generally. Fortunately or unfortunately, Bart was quite attractive physically, and so had always been able to escape from his self-doubts through sexual adventures with women.

Betty's family history was about 90 degrees different from Bart's. (If it had been 180 degrees, or totally opposite, they might have had an easier time understanding one another!) In her family, where she was the eldest of three girls, there was little, if any, emotional upheaval. In fact, her parents showed almost no emotion, as far as Betty could recall. She felt the family was especially lacking in the sharing of physical affection. Thus, while Betty deeply wished for a life of emotional contact and physical affection, she was ill-prepared for it and secretly doubted that she could have this in her life (since she had not had it during the years when her self-image was in its formative stages). Betty's parents never showed affection or anger to one another, at least in front of the children. Betty learned to get attention by being smart in school, but since high achievement came easily to her, she was not driven in this area.

Neither of Betty's parents were particularly powerful or worldly, but neither were they particularly weak. Betty did have a feeling that their life was a bit boring, however, and she vowed at an early age that her marriage would be more exciting. Still, her formative experiences with marriage were associated with a somewhat emotionally detached style of being rather than anything very demanding.

Bart had known emotional closeness in his early life and had experienced mainly its costs. Betty had never felt such emotional closeness, and longed for it. Thus, his tendency to feel smothered and her high need for contact. When they were in love, they had been able to accommodate to their differences and give the other what each needed. But once in a state of disappointment, the zest for such sacrifice seemed lost. Behavior that is perfectly natural and appropriate during the Romance Stage of a relationship often just won't work during the Power Struggle Stage.*

The counselor began to probe Betty and Bart for reactions both to the inclusive-exclusive disagreement and the *meaning* each placed upon the other's behavior. New dimensions of their differences began to come to the surface.

For Bart, having other sex partners meant that he was not being controlled or dominated as he had been earlier by his father and his sister. It was also a way of staving off doubts and fears about his self-worth.

---

*See *The Couple's Journey* for a fuller treatment of the stages of relationship.

For Betty, Bart's being sexual with other women meant that he was not really emotionally invested in her — just as she felt her parents had not been. She felt that Bart feared emotional closeness and would never be able to give her what she had lacked and therefore now needed in her life.

Neither of them saw that for Bart, emotional closeness was nothing new and therefore no big thing, just as for Betty, high achievement was so familiar that it had lost its motivating power. Each could see the pitfalls in the path that had always been familiar, but neither could see the partner's viewpoint.

This brings us to the next step in the process of resolving a power struggle. After differences and disagreements are fully examined, it is time to expand each person's perspective to include the other side. Sometimes this occurs simply through the understanding that comes from exchanging life stories and meaning systems. In this instance, however, both Bart and Betty needed to actually *experience* their other sides, the sides of themselves they had never fully expressed.

Betty, never having experienced really intense emotion, especially anger, needed to feel this aspect of herself in order to really understand Bart. He, in turn, had never been able to feel another's emotions without being controlled by them, and needed to experience himself as both autonomous and responsive to another's feelings. Betty and Bart needed to learn a new way to fight — instead of acting out their struggle via the open-vs. closed-marriage issue.

The counselor coached Betty first in how to express anger, starting with an acknowledgement of the anger she felt toward her parents for ignoring her needs for affection. As Bart observed Betty's angry emotions from a safe distance (since they were not directed at him), he was able to emotionally respond to her without feeling his autonomy was at stake. The counselor helped Bart to move his attention first closer to and then more distant from identification with Betty's feelings, at his own rhythm. This helped him to see that he could voluntarily feel another's emotional need without being controlled by it.

When Betty had learned not to fear her angry side and was able to accept this in herself, she was then ready to express her anger and hurt directly to Bart. She showed a willingness to have her anger taken seriously rather than hiding her feelings behind a shield of niceness as she asserted, "Bart, it hurts me deeply when you choose to be with another woman when you know how much I want to be with you!"

This gave Bart some information he hadn't had before — the fact that Betty *wanted* him. He countered with "If you *say* you want me, I'd like you to show it! Act like you care about me rather than hiding behind that victim facade. You won't fight for what you want. You just automatically declare yourself a loser!"

At this remark, Betty burst into tears, yet was able to speak clearly in spite of them, "You're right," she acknowledged, "or you're right about how I *was*. But I'm fighting for what I want *now,* and I don't intend to give up. You're worth swallowing my pride for. I do feel silly acting so emotional, but I don't care. It's the first time I've really let myself want someone. And you're that someone."

Bart smiled and softened, saying simply, "It's about time."

In this dialogue, we can see how, if one partner makes a move toward abandoning pride and expressing softer feelings, it is a lot more likely that the other will do the same. Each one is looking for reassurance that he or she is loved and accepted. When this reassurance occurs, a natural softening takes place.

In Bart and Betty's situation, Betty's strong expression of anger was seen by Bart as taking a risk and "*showing* how much she really cared about me instead of just *talking* about it." This event helped Bart see Betty in a way that he had not been able to see a woman in the past. He was able to see that "all women are not all-suffering and willing to put up with anything a man dishes out.... That gave me a new respect for Betty and in a funny sort of way, for myself, too."

Bart was then able to admit the fact that he had probably been trying to provoke Betty's anger by advocating an open marriage. He had also been testing out his own sense of autonomy, and had found that even when Betty was putting intense pressure on him to see things her way, he had still felt a sense of choice. He realized therefore that avoiding involvement and confrontation is not the royal road to autonomy, that one's sense of autonomy comes more from being able to honestly express one's feelings than from always having one's way.

As it turned out, Bart's wish for other sex partners was his way of bringing to light some conflicts that had been buried in his relationship with Betty. What he really wanted was for Betty to tell him when she was angry or disappointed, rather than to withdraw her responsiveness by playing the victim. If she could stay open and responsive to him by confronting rather than stifling her feelings, then there was hope that she might be "enough for him" sexually.

Bart also saw that his over-involvement in his work, as well as his tendency to look toward other women for satisfaction, were parts of his own long-standing way of dealing with difficult emotions. When he felt unloved, he would look outside the relationship rather than toward Betty. Now that Betty had taken a risk in his direction, however, he felt moved to risk putting more of himself *into* the relationship also. He confessed to Betty, "When you confront me like that, it makes me feel important, which was something I guess I was trying to get from my work and from other women...I still plan to put a lot into my work, but I don't think I'll be so compulsive about it if you'll keep reminding me to relax."

Betty, of course, wanted also to know how Bart now felt about opening the marriage, to which he replied, "I was trying to get to a feeling that I now see I can have with you without going to other sex partners, a feeling of aliveness. When you were sitting on your anger and I was over-working, our sex life felt dead to me. Now, we've come to life again, and I don't need to look elsewhere."

Often in a relationship, one partner will be more attuned than the other to the quality of aliveness present between them. This partner will often try to get the other's attention in various ways, usually gently at first. But if these gentler, subtler ways don't have an impact, often this person will do something to actively provoke a crisis. In the case of Bart and Betty, it was Bart who provoked the crisis. But it was Betty who made the first move toward opening and softening. Thus, it takes cooperation to weather a relationship crisis. At several points, their marriage could have gone either way. It was mainly due to the support each was willing to give when the other showed some vulnerability that led to the happy resolution of this crisis.

## Why Co-Workers Fight

Just as marriage and intimate relationships provide fertile ground for dealing with feelings about loveability, so the world of work offers a rich environment for focusing on one's competence and creativity.

Fights in the workplace often revolve around different ways to do a job. The disagreements that cause the most problems are those with a supervisor or boss. It is in relation to someone in authority that people tend to feel most vulnerable (and often therefore, most open to learning). Bosses often re-stimulate feelings first experienced in the family while growing up. If we pick spouses who can be our mirrors and our teachers — perhaps our ''choice'' of bosses (no matter how accidental it may seem) also reflects our drive toward growth and wholeness.

*Matt Hinkley's Authority Problem* — Matt Hinkley was a 36-year-old computer programmer in a large high-tech organization. Matt had grown up in an achievement-oriented family, the youngest of three sons. During his early school years, Matt felt he was continually being compared to his very intelligent older brothers, by his teachers as well as by his parents. Believing there was no way he could match their accomplishments, he withdrew his energies from school and put them into tinkering with mechanical things. His parents failed to see value in his tinkering and were constantly after him to do his homework and to get better grades in school. He learned to get attention by being a procrastinator. He also learned that others would interfere with his freedom if he let them, so he developed the habit of listening to advice or direction, and then ignoring it.

The self-image and habits Matt developed as a child were reflected now in his relationship with his boss. The more Ray Falzone pressured him to meet a deadline, the slower he went. Ray was the type of boss who liked to keep a close watch over his employees. He would give very detailed instructions when giving an assignment — a style which went totally counter to Matt's preferred way of working. Matt felt pressured and controlled, just as he had felt with his parents during childhood.

"Ever since I can remember," pondered Matt, "my parents, teachers, and bosses have been after me to hurry up.... I wonder if there's a lesson in this for me."

Matt's curiosity about his lesson seems appropriate. He had noticed a recurring pattern in his life, a recurring power struggle with those in authority over him. He began to question what he might learn from the situation, so that he could stop attracting this sort of problem.

Resolution of Matt's recurring struggle with authority needs to start with recognition of his *inner* conflicts. Such internal struggles are mirrored in external conflict with others. Matt still carries in his head the voices of the authority figures of his youth. We are all products of our early years, of course, but Matt too often allows those voices to dominate the other aspects of his personality. This causes an inner struggle between the *youthful* Matt — who wants freedom from control — and the *parental* Matt — who wants to make sure youthful Matt does the right thing.

If Matt Hinkley, the adult, is to learn the lesson being offered in his current work situation, he will need to find a new more equal relationship between his youthful and parental sides. He will need, for example, to get his two sides ''communicating'' with each other in an attitude of mutual respect rather than resentment and mistrust. But first, he will need to stop blaming others for the predicaments in which he finds himself. It is not his boss who is causing his difficulty at work. It is the fact that Matt has not yet come into a respectful relationship to his *inner* authority. He has associated authority and initiative with domination and over-control, and has thus never been motivated to *become an authority* in his own life, the author of his own life script.

Here is an excerpt from a typical meeting between Matt and Ray which illustrates the pattern:

*Ray* (who always initiates their contacts, always has the first word): Come on in, Matt. Sit down.

*Matt* (responsively): Hi Ray, how are you?

*Ray* (who likes to get down to business right away): I want you to take over the maintenance and supervision of all sick leave records. Do you think you can handle that?

*Matt* (already getting defensive): What do you mean, can I handle it?

*Ray* (trying to stick to the task at hand): Of course you can handle it. Now, here's how I'd like things done: On Monday, you'll get the files from Personnel. Paul Blakely is the man to contact there. Then call my secretary, Sharon, and tell her exactly how many entries there will be for this month. We may need to revise our keypunch process. On Tuesday, I want you to check on the procedures used in payroll to make sure your system is compatible with theirs.

*Matt* (who has been feeling tight in the chest since Ray began speaking): Uh, okay, sure. Anything else?

This dialogue shows clearly who is using his inner authority and who is not. Matt's behavior shows him to be more of a follower than an initiator. And although he would like to re-direct the course of the conversation, he seems incapable of doing so. He behaves as if the course is pre-determined and no input by him can possibly have any influence. As a result, he feels small and powerless in relationship to Ray — just as he always did with his parents.

If we consider the relationship of Matt and Ray in terms of the Polar Dimensions discussed in chapter three, it is easy to see that Matt is a Lover and Ray a Warrior.

Perhaps Matt's parents did ignore or punish his early attempts to influence them. And perhaps Matt gave up trying to be heard at an early age. But his *need* to be heard did not disappear — only his expression of that need. In place of such expression, we now find resentment and subtle resistance to direction by others.

To overcome such a self-defeating pattern, Matt must first see his behavior as something he is voluntarily doing — not as something others are making him do. If he can see how he is "playing second" — always fitting in to what's already given — he can perhaps also see other options for himself. He might begin by mentally replaying the above dialogue and looking for places where he could have re-directed the course of things. He could have responded to Ray's question, "Do you think you can handle that?" with something more assertive, such as: "Let me tell you how I would handle it and see what you think."

With such an approach, Matt would be setting the stage and asking Ray to reply in a particular manner, rather than the other way around. Matt is taking the initiative, inviting Ray to respond, while remaining open to Ray's response. He is taking charge of the situation without dominating. Once he can see viable ways to be in authority without being over-controlling, perhaps he can more easily allow himself to express his own needs for control (rather than projecting them onto the boss).

To overcome a self-defeating pattern such as Matt's, it takes a willingness to let go of one's negative self-image and try something new. It requires also a willingness to feel awkward, simply because one is treading in new territory. Old habits, even if they are blatantly self-defeating, are somehow comfortable and therefore resistant to change. Thus, Matt will need to be really fed up with this habit pattern if he is to sustain the motivation to express and develop his inner authority.

What generally occurs when a person like Matt begins to assert more authority in relationship to a boss is that the boss tends to gradually back down and to assume less control. There may be a transition period of awkwardness, confusion, or even resistance, but in time the balance of power shifts toward more equality. Of course, this can only occur if the *inner* balance of power for the individuals is undergoing a similar shift. And, in my experience, it doesn't matter which comes first — the inner change or the outer. Either one can set the process in motion, for both parties, even if only one of them has the intention to change.

As Matt becomes more authoritative, the stage is set for Ray to feel the other side of his coin — his ability to listen, to follow, to be responsive to another. There will usually be a transition period of ambiguity as newer aspects of Matt's and Ray's personalities come to know and trust one another. But after a time, they may find that both have a fuller range of responses available in the relationship. This brings more aliveness and creativity into their contacts.

While Matt's struggle with Ray was never overt, it nevertheless had all the qualities of a classic power struggle: a difference in viewpoint; an inability to accept this difference as a matter of course; an interpretation of this difference as a threat to the relationship or to the self-esteem of one or both people; a difficulty being open with one another due to lack of inner harmony or self-acceptance.

In the ideal work relationship, as in the ideal love relationship, there is an ever-expanding quality of aliveness. It is not so important that Matt be the fully self-aware employee or Ray, the fully mature boss. What seems to be more important for overall health and happiness is a relationship where there is opportunity for expansion through

the open confrontation of differences — where struggle leads
to a gradually increasing self-understanding.

## How Interdependence Contributes to Friction

Some lifestyles provide more fertile ground than others
for potential power struggles. Generally speaking, the more
*interdependent* the partners are, the more difference their
differences will make.

A couple which shares one income or pools all its
financial resources will face more opportunity for joint
decision-making than a couple which maintains two separate
bank accounts. Family or group members sharing a small
house, a camper, or a live-aboard yacht will rub up against
one another more often than those sharing a larger home.

An organizational structure where each department is
responsible for supporting and disbursing its own budget will
foster less conflict than one where all departments must
procure resources from a single source. A husband and wife
who are sexually monogamous will find a greater need to
harmonize their differences in rhythm and preference than
will a couple which is non-monogamous.

A highly interdependent relationship may foster more
friction and conflict than one which offers more independence
of movement and decision-making. Yet people usually learn
more and grow more in situations characterized by more
rather than less interdependence. In other words, it may hurt,
but it'll probably be good for you!

The price of such growth may be too high, however. I
knew a couple who argued constantly about money, almost to
the point of break-up, until they decided to maintain separate
bank accounts. After that they got along fine. This is an
example of a change in the partners' *financial*
interdependence. Such a change may occur while still
maintaining a high degree of sexual interdependence
(monogamy) or spatial interdependence (living in a small
place). Thus, you can change your friction potential in one
area of your life without changing other areas.

Each of us must choose our battles in this life according to our individual values; some areas are worth fighting about and some are not. Some people, because of their particular life journey, need to learn about money and finances, others about sexual togetherness or freedom, and others about sharing a physical territory. Life has a mysterious way of presenting us with those lessons which we need to learn, so don't be too eager to escape the friction you encounter.

I recently found myself in a situation which confronted me with my need for physical space and which showed me the close parallel between the need for physical space and the need for emotional space.

For most of my life I have lived in large houses with spacious yards, where I had at least one good-sized room of my own and often an entire house to myself. All that came to an end when my husband and I decided to live aboard a 47-foot sailboat in preparation for a year-long cruise to the South Pacific.

Both of us are big people physically and like to move around a lot. In addition, I am an aerobic dance addict and need room to jump around to the accompaniment of loud music at least once a day. The actual floor space aboard our boat was less than 60 square feet. So it was impossible for me to dance without comandeering the boat's entire interior for the duration of my workout. When our boat was at anchor, if my husband didn't feel like being a voluntary or involuntary participant in my aerobic session, he had very few options. He could go for a swim or take a ride in the dinghy. Since I felt it unfair for one person to dominate all the boat's available space, I began more and more to restrict my dancing to periods when he was away from the boat. As a result, I began to feel crowded by him and constricted by our living quarters.

Before long I was experiencing a pervasive sense of claustrophobia, expressed in frequently recurring impulses to jump off the boat for a long swim or to row to shore for long solitary walks. I indulged these impulses one or more times a day for over a month. But even such expansive behavior as this did not alleviate my sense of being crowded.

While all this was taking place, I also began to notice that my husband and I had stopped talking to one another, except when absolutely necessary. It was as if we were already seeing more than enough of each other without increasing the stress by direct contact.

We both read quite a few novels during that time aboard the boat, until finally I started to feel lonely. I realized we had created an *emotional* gulf between us as a compensation for our needs for *physical* space. Instead of finding ways to create a mutually satisfying sense of physical spaciousness on the boat, we had opted to create emotional distance.

With the recognition of this situation came a willingness to talk openly about our needs for physical space and a feeling of great relief. We both admitted that we had felt a bit timid and even somewhat guilty about expressing needs for separateness; we had adopted this lifestyle in part because of the sense of intimacy it would foster.

Once we could recognize and name the problem, solving it was easy. In talking it over, for example, we found that there was at least one period each day when he didn't mind loud music because the boat was noisy anyway. That was the time during which he had to run the engine in order to charge our boat's batteries. We also discovered that we both had a need for quiet in the evening, but that quiet didn't necessarily mean alone, each buried in our separate novels. We found that lying together quietly holding one another was a nourishing way to achieve the restful peace that we sought after the day's activity.

As we talked about our needs for privacy and independence in our highly interdependent environment, we were able to devise ways of making our little home feel much more spacious. In addition to resolving our power struggle over physical space, the greater satisfaction was in learning that more than half of the solution was in openly acknowledging the problem.

The friction of a highly interdependent lifestyle need not lead to struggle — unless partners resist facing the unavoidable need to *communicate* about their differences!

# eight: Your Thoughts Make a Difference

**Imagine this scene:** You and the person you live with are accustomed to sharing dinner together every evening at about 7 p.m. Tonight, however, your partner has not arrived home by the usual hour. You are concerned but, after waiting a while, go ahead and have dinner alone. In your mind you scan all the possible things that could have occurred to make your partner late. You decide against calling friends or the police because this type of thing has happened before on rare occasions and always with a reason.

Late in the evening, still having no word from your partner, you go on to bed. At about 2 a.m., you hear a rustling about in the kitchen. You go downstairs and find your partner sitting at the table munching on a cheese sandwich. What do you think? What do you feel? And what do you say?

Many people imagine the worst when such things occur. She's been having an affair; he's been in an accident; he's involved in something illegal; she's trying to provoke me into ending it.

Other people try to make light of the whole situation, as if questioning the partner about it would be a symbol of ill will or lack of trust. They deny their concern and reassure

113

themselves that everything is okay now that the partner has returned.

Still others respond somewhere in between these two extremes. They talk about their concern and ask what happened, without jumping to conclusions.

An unexpected event can move you in one of several ways. You can overreact as if it's the worst thing that could ever happen, an unforgiveable sin. You can underreact and forgive your partner without question, preferring to ignore the situation rather than confront your partner. Or you can reserve judgement, keeping an open mind and seeking to learn what actually happened.

How you respond to an event such as this is a matter of choice. Unfortunately, the choices most of us make are based on such a mixture of conscious and unconscious factors as to afford very little *real* choice in the matter. Nevertheless, it is useful to pay attention to our behavior under such conditions; it reveals much about our beliefs and assumptions regarding how people are and how the world works.

## The Security/Control Mode of Coping

Perhaps you deal with a situation such as a loved one coming home late by assuming you know what has happened, without needing to wait and see. Maybe your assumptions tend toward the catastrophic: "She doesn't care about me anymore!" Or they may be anastrophic: "He's out with my friends planning a surprise party for me." Or you may try to overlook the incident: "I know he loves me, and that's all that really matters."

All three of these assumptions, regardless of their apparent dissimilarity, are attempts to maintain a sense of control over a situation that is potentially threatening to one's security. To avoid feeling helpless and vulnerable, people often jump to conclusions about why the other person did what he or she did, when in fact they are relying on inference and imagination. Whether one assumes the worst or the best, there is still a certain rigidity in this style of coping. The person armors against the unexpected, rather than experience the uncertainty of not knowing. Beneath this coping style, there seems to be an assumption that the world is basically an unfriendly place; otherwise why do I need to arm myself for protection?

The Security/Control style of coping often stems from one or more incidents in early childhood or infancy, in which the person experienced pain while being open, loving or trusting, or while under the care or authority of someone inconsistent and erratic. "Miss Goodie Two Shoes," whom we met in an earlier chapter, is an example of this latter situation. As a consequence of such early environmental influences, Patricia learned to protect her emotional sensitivity and maintain a sense of invulnerability by staying in control of herself and her environment as much as possible. Such a child grows up with the attitude that it is a better, more secure position to know how things will turn out than to not know. Uncertainty, unpredictability and ambiguity are avoided because they remind the person of the anxiety of her earlier life. Thus, much of her behavior becomes centered around maintaining a sense of security through control, manipulation, the search for certainty and the avoidance of pain or disappointment.

The basic credo of the Security/Control mode of coping is: "I maintain my sense of well-being by trying to stay in control of myself and my surroundings." This credo will lead a person to maintain at least an illusion of control in ambiguous situations, such as the lateness example: "Look, don't bother to explain. I know she had long blond hair and was about five-foot-two and slinky! If you ever do that again without calling me, we're finished. That's all I have to say. Don't insult me with your reasons and excuses. And don't try to comfort me. I will not be comforted!" The Security/Control position aims at controlling one's own feelings and reactions so as not to be vulnerable to upset. It also aims at controlling the other's behavior in an attempt to create for oneself a stable, predictable environment.

## The Growth/Discovery Position

Another way of coping with an unexpected, potentially upsetting situation is to stay open to all possibilities. Since you do not *know* what happened, it can be helpful to attempt to understand what did happen and why. In this stance the essential values are to know and be known by the other person. The aim is understanding, not control. And the vehicles are self-disclosure and openness to hearing the other's position. In the lateness situation, a person might ask, "What happened to make you so late? I was expecting you at seven. I wish you'd called me. I was concerned."

Here, the aim of the communication is to know and be known. The stance is straight and open, grounded in one's own feelings. It does not bend over backward to comfort or appease the other; nor does it move forward too quickly into drawing conclusions about the other's motives.

The Growth/Discovery position is based on the assumption that the world is friendly and that symbiotic cooperation is part of the nature of all living things. People who hold this attitude trust that the more understanding you have, the more at home you'll feel with life. Thus, new knowledge or information is to be welcomed rather than avoided. Whereas the Security/Control stance avoids new information for fear it will be hurtful or unsettling, the Growth/Discovery attitude welcomes even disappointing information because it helps one see reality more clearly. Such an attitude generally comes from an early environment that was loving, trustworthy and reliable, or from a decision later in life to open oneself to the ever-changing newness of life, even though this may at times bring pain.

It often happens that a person will live a good portion of life in the Security/Control position before realizing how limiting it is. At this point, the person may make a conscious decision to live in a way that is more welcoming to life's vagaries. The idea here is to grow in understanding of oneself and others and also in one's ability to respond flexibly in a wide range of situations.

The basic credo of this constellation of motives, the Growth/Discovery position, is, "I grow and discover the true nature of things by being open to experiencing what is occurring in and around me." In this stance there is a drive to discover and express one's latent talents and feelings. Novelty, variety and unpredictability are valued because situations which offer such novelty also challenge one to develop new modes of coping. The coming-home-late situation might thus be valued as a potential stimulus to personal growth and deeper understanding in the relationship. Here, one realizes that pain and crisis can be symptoms that something needs to change.

## The Unity/Participation Position

There is a third set of assumptions from which behavior often arises. I call this the Unity/Participation position. Here one feels no separation between oneself and others or the environment. The world is not seen as friendly or unfriendly. Instead, one is simply a participating part of the world. One belongs to a *we-system* in couple relationship, or to the *corpus humani* in relationship to the world. One's attention is focused not so much on oneself as an individual, but on the whole world and oneself as a part of it. One seeks to become attuned to the environment, much like the strings of a guitar are tuned so that they will vibrate together with a harmonious resonance. A further goal is to contribute to one's surroundings in beneficial ways, such as to inject humor where there has been tension, or insight where there has been confusion.

The Unity/Participation attitude is one of intuitive empathy and understanding of others, often without verbal communication. This is the person who knows what is needed in a situation and is neither afraid to take action nor to let things alone, depending upon what the moment calls for. In the coming-home-late situation, the Unity/Participation person knows that the other feels a need to explain, and simply remains available to listen with open, undistracted

attention. There is no special concern with obtaining any
particular outcome; one is oriented more toward *loving what
one has* than toward *getting what one wants*.

While it is not common in our culture, there are many
people who do hold this attitude, usually after many years of
deep spiritual work. There are many religious, spiritual or
philosophical traditions which support this stance, and
adherents often belong to a group or network of like-minded
others. Since this position is so far from the norm of today's
society, some sort of support system is often needed to help
one sustain such an attitude.

## How Attitudes Affect Outcomes

Security/Control, Growth/discovery, and Unity/
Participation offer three different perspectives on life.
Security/Control is a close-up, with emphasis on your own
comfort and security. Growth/Discovery is a mid-range view,
and includes other people and information. Unity/
Participation is the broadest and longest-range perspective —
an aerial photo of your relationship to all of life. You can see
everything, but you do not identify too closely with any of it.

While no one is entirely consistent in adopting one
perspective or another, most of us do find one of the three
positions more comfortable or more compatible with our own
needs and goals.

Each perspective leads to a different set of assumptions
about life and relationships. And very different styles of
behavior follow from those assumptions, especially in a crisis.
Viewed at close range, a situation may seem quite urgent.
Viewed from a greater distance, more complexities can be
seen, and rigid or pat solutions are rejected. Viewed from
afar, people and events are seen in perspective, and actions
are likely to respond to the needs of the larger whole.

Attitudes powerfully influence behavior, and the three
life perspectives I have described have strong effects on
action. In any given situation, even an unexpected crisis, you

can choose the life view which will serve you best. You may not be able to control what happens to you very well, but you can choose your responses to what happens. You can, for example, "zoom" to a long range view and keep life events in perspective. A powerful instance of this principle is given in the autobiography, *Man's Search for Meaning,* by the German psychiatrist Victor Frankl.

In this book, Dr. Frankl recounts his several years as a prisoner in a Nazi concentration camp during World War II. Frankl's daily existence in the camp compelled him to witness the most horrifying and unthinkable inhumanities inflicted upon his fellow Jews. Each day at dawn when Frankl heard the stiff, heavy footsteps of the Nazi guards, he knew there would be a list of names summoning a large number of prisoners to the maximum security area, where they would be stripped of their clothing and possessions, searched in every part of their bodies for concealed valuables, herded like animals into crowded cells, gassed to death, and then incinerated. Every evening as he lay on his blanket trying to sleep, Frankl could smell the abominable odor emanating from the ovens. He lived with the constant knowledge that some morning when the guard marched in shouting off names from the list, his name might be among those called.

Frankl soon realized the impossibility of dealing with such a situation using his normal repertoire of responses. It was then that he decided that, in spite of the horror he felt about what was taking place around him, he would never lose his spirit of good will and compassion. The guards could bully him or beat him, but his inner attitude would always remain calm and forgiving. He would do what was necessary to appease his keepers, but he would not let their insults poison his self-respect.

Frankl knew his salvation as a human being rested in maintaining his sense of choice. He could not control the external events of his life, but he could choose his feelings and attitudes. He chose to look beyond the effect of immediate events on his personal well-being and instead focused his concern on the larger question of what it means to be a human being, and on what might be the meaning of human suffering. He saw the pain and suffering that he and his fellows were forced to endure as a means of learning life's deepest lessons, not as something to be resented or avoided. And when the armistice came, and he was set free, he did not forget the lessons he had learned nor the attitude with which he had learned them.

Reading this account of one man's victory over fear and hatred, one cannot help wondering if perhaps his calm outlook was one reason he was allowed to live. Maybe his serenity had a positive effect on the camp which was felt by the guards or their fuhrers. Or perhaps what he had discovered about living made him an especially valuable resource in the world.

We can only speculate about such things; but we can use such speculation as a stimulus for experimentation in our own lives. We can watch what happens to us when we are radiating negative energy as a result of harboring fearful or hostile thoughts. And we can likewise observe the changes that occur in our outer lives when we change our thoughts.

## The Power of Your Thoughts

In my life, I've seen time and again how fears come true. It is a little harder to make dreams come true, I'm sorry to say. But fears seem to have a magnetic power which is unexcelled in the world of emotions. People who continually worry about money wind up feeling poor, no matter what their bank balance. People who worry about the regularity of their bowel movements are the ones who always seem to be constipated. People who worry about losing their lover to someone else often find themselves being left. It is a strange but familiar phenomenon how our fears seem to haunt us, often growing stronger the more we seek to avoid them.

A recurring fear in my own life is the fear of being used by others for their own selfish interests. I inherited this fear from my parents, who I remember often cautioning me to beware of life's freeloaders, of people who take more out of life's pot than they put into it. These people will take from you and give little in return.

What my parents didn't know was that within most people there are tendencies to freeload and tendencies toward generosity. And circumstances have a lot to do with which of these tendencies will manifest at any given time or in any particular relationship. A very important circumstance to be considered is the quality of the relationship, the degree to which it is characterized by a fear-based vs. an open attitude; that is, by a Security/Control vs. a Growth/Discovery or Unity/Participation perspective.

I have frequently observed that when I approach a potential friend or lover with suspicion, paying particular attention to how he always takes and rarely gives, he comes to view himself that way when he is in my presence. If instead, I overlook his selfishness and call attention to his generosity, he actually becomes more giving toward me. The best way to overcome this fear of being used is to allow another to give to me; but as long as I critically minimize his gifts, they will remain minimal. If I can truly appreciate the generosities he does show me, my mistrust diminishes and his generosity expands.

All this occurs because people are incredibly interdependent psychically. We influence one another's self-concepts and actions more than we know. Back in the mid-1960's, Kenneth Clark and his colleagues did extensive research on the self-concepts of Black children in the New York City schools. They found that when a teacher had negative expectations of a child's ability, that child would generally perform less well than when he was in the classroom with a teacher who had a higher estimation of his abilities.

We are all a bit like the teachers in Clark's research, constantly creating environments for each other that are conducive to success or failure, generosity or free-loading. If I relate to my partner from the Security/Control-dominated part of myself, he is likely to behave in ways that reinforce my needs for security and control.

When I exercise the Growth/Discovery attitude, I'm not attached to his doing things in a particular way. Thus, I will reap growth and discovery almost no matter what he does. In this model of the world, everything that occurs in my relationships can help me achieve greater self-understanding, regardless of whether it pleases or displeases me.

If my Unity/Participation aspect is in the foreground in my thoughts, everything that my partner does is seen as appropriate. In the Growth/Discovery position, if I felt resistant to another's behavior I could use that resistance to help me see myself more clearly. In the Unity/Participation world, I rarely experience resistance. Unity/Participation may be considered the most fully *both-and*, or inclusive, of the three attitudes.

It is understandable that my partner might react differently toward me depending upon whether I am:

— using him to bolster my own sense of security or power; trying to control him

— accepting what he does as beyond my control and as a stimulus for my growth and learning; celebrating his uniqueness

— empathizing with his feelings and actions; appreciating their absolute rightness in the overall larger scheme of things, beyond how they affect me personally.

The more open, less fearful, I can be regarding another's relationship to me, the more this will tend to open the other to me and my needs. Of course, there are many, many factors governing any situation, openness being only one factor.

While we cannot *control* the events that happen to us, we can and do, by our thoughts and beliefs, exert a real *influence* on such events.

In addition to this "mental" influence on what seem to be "external" events, our beliefs affect to an even greater degree our own feelings of acceptance or resistance. When I believe my partner intends to use me selfishly, I will tend to resist him and the situation no matter what he does, and I will feel generally tense in his presence. This makes it unlikely

that I will learn or receive anything new in the situation.
When I believe he is supportive of me, I will feel relaxed in his
presence and open to learning and receiving from him.

Beliefs and assumptions affect all aspects of
relationships. It appears that we would do well to respect the
power of our thoughts.

## Reader Participation Activity

As you read through the scenes described below,
imagine first your immediate gut reaction to each situation. Is
it based more on a security-oriented attitude, a
growth-oriented attitude, or a unity-oriented attitude?

Then try to imagine an entirely different way to handle
the same situation. If your first reaction was to seek security
and control, imagine how you might respond if your aim was
growth and learning. If you automatically operated out of a
Unity/Participation posture, see if you can picture yourself in
a Security/Control stance.

The goal here is self-discovery and flexibility, not fitting
everyone into some ideal mold. Admittedly I feel that the
Growth/Discovery and Unity/Participation attitudes are more
conducive to harmony and long-range happiness; but I also
feel there are times when the Security/Control attitude is
necessary. Even when it may not be necessary, we must all
own up to the security and control-oriented aspects of our
personalities so that we do not project these attitudes onto
others, causing more problems than if we acted them out
ourselves.

Please don't take yourself too seriously during this
activity. See yourself as an actor learning to play the same
scene two or three different ways. Only when you have a
sense of your own flexibility can you feel truly free.

After you have gone through all the scenes that interest
you, begin to reflect back on whether you noticed a pattern or
habitual tendency in your responses. Do you rather
consistently adopt one set of assumptions more easily than
the others? Do you tend, for example, to make it easy or

difficult for another person to approach you? How do you achieve this? With posture? Eye contact? Words? What results does this usually bring you? Are you satisfied with these results? Were you able to imagine things turning out differently when you adopted a different basic attitude?

Scenes are presented in three sections:
— those portraying singles and people who have not previously met
— those portraying married persons
— those portraying co-workers.

## Singles

*Laundromat*     You're folding your freshly laundered sheets and towels at your neighborhood laundromat. As you look up from what you're doing, your eyes meet with a person of the opposite sex who is across the room unloading clothes from the dryer. You look deeply and intently into one another's eyes for a brief instant that seems like an eternity. Then, your new "acquaintance" smiles warmly, looks back at the clothes, and continues unloading.

You feel a strong attraction to this person — stronger than you've felt for anyone in a very long time.

What, if anything, do you do? What thoughts and feelings run through your mind? What, if any, assumptions do you make?

*Party*     You're at a party talking to someone you've just met and find quite attractive. You sense a genuine mutual rapport, and after a while, you suggest, "Why don't we get together sometime for lunch or something?" The other person seems genuinely interested. You talk a bit more and then the other person leaves to go to the bathroom. You go and get some food, and when you return, your new friend is talking to someone else. What do you assume, feel, do?

*Sex*    You've been dating T. at least once weekly for several months now, and the two of you seem to be growing to care for each other more and more. You have felt for the past 2 or 3 weeks that you'd like to have sex with T., but so far you have not done anything to indicate or express this.

     The next time you're out with T., the two of you go to dinner and a movie. On the way back to T.'s place, T. complains of a headache.

     What do you do, say, think, feel, assume?

*Work*    You've been working in the same company with S. for two years. You've always been attracted, but since S. was married up until a few months ago, you never thought a romantic relationship possible. Now that you've learned of S.'s divorce, you're secretly elated at the prospect of perhaps beginning to go out together.

     Your office Christmas dance is coming up in two weeks, so one day during a coffee break, you gently suggest that newly-single S. might like a companion for the evening.

     S. seems surprised at your suggestion, and says, "No, I don't think that would be a good idea." Then S. smiles very warmly and says, "Thanks for asking me, though."

     What do you do then/next? What do you think, feel, assume?

*Date*    You're out with M. (Someone you feel only a mild attraction to) for the second time, having a drink at a local nightspot. M. seems preoccupied, so you ask, "What's on your mind, M.?" After a long pause, M. says, "I was just thinking how much I'd like us to go home and make love."

     What do you say, do, feel, think?

## Married Persons

*Kids*    It's past the usual bedtime for your children and you're trying to get them to go to bed. Just when you feel you've almost got them convinced, your spouse comes into

the room and shouts at you, ''I'm trying to read in here! Why
don't you just leave them alone?!''
     What do you do, say, think, feel?

*Support*          You've been noticing that your spouse often
seems preoccupied with something else just when you need
his/her attention most. This is beginning to bother you a
great deal.
     One day when you're feeling especially in need of
support, you ask your mate for a hand with the vacuuming.
The response is an unenthusiastic, ''Not now honey, I'm
busy.''
     What do you think, feel, say, do?

*T.V.*          You and your spouse are sitting next to each other on
the couch watching T.V. At the commercial, your partner
moves closer to you and starts stroking your thigh.
     What do you think, feel, do?

*Past Lovers*          Your spouse has a habit of recalling fond
memories of past lovers in your presence. You find this less
than appealing.
     What do you think, feel, do, say?

## Co-Workers

*Employee Development*          One day, your boss calls you into
the office with what seems to be a friendlier-than-usual
attitude. Here's the pitch: ''I've got an opportunity for you!
Have you ever heard of the Radvine Institute? ... Well, they
offer employee development programs — programs where
you can learn how to improve your communications skills and
interpersonal relations. And we have money budgeted for two
of our employees to go to their week-long December training
program. I'm strongly recommending to Personnel that you
be one of those two from this company. (Pause) I feel it's
important to your job that you go. How about it?''

What do you think, feel, say? What assumptions do you make about your boss's reasons for recommending that you do this?

*Performance Review*    It's time for you to give semi-annual performance reviews to the six people working for you. One of your employees, Max, is performing somewhat below par, but more significant than this is his attitude. Max does all jobs to the minimum of your requirements. He seems never to expend more than the minimum effort necessary.

At the appointed hour, Max comes into your office, looking somewhat sullen.

What feelings and thoughts are going on within you as you greet Max? How do you handle the review with Max?

*Job Assignment*    You and your boss seem to have very different styles of working. He keeps a lot of projects going on all at once, does everything very rapidly, and tends to make many errors as a result. You prefer to do things more slowly and thoroughly.

Today, the boss calls you in to give you an assignment: "This time I'll only ask you to do half what I usually ask of you, because you seem to be under some kind of strain. The jobs you'll be responsible for this quarter are (—·), (—·), (—·), and (—·)." You believe each of the four jobs could easily take the full allotted time.

What do you feel and think?

How do you respond?

*Feedback*    You've just finished an important piece of work, one that you feel may affect the future of your career. And, although you feel that you did a good job, you're not sure how your boss will evaluate it. In the past, your boss has not been a person to offer feedback very easily or readily. Thus, you have a hard time knowing where you stand.

Just as you're thinking these thoughts, your boss comes up to your workspace and asks, "Well, is it done yet?"

How do you respond?
What other feelings and thoughts occur to you?

# nine: Relationship Struggle Reflects Inner Struggle

Joel is unhappy in his relationship with Janet because she doesn't trust him to be financially responsible. He resents her frequent complaints that he never remembers when bills are due. She says she always has to come to the rescue to avoid foreclosures and the ruination of their credit rating. He feels angry and misunderstood whenever Janet begins her critical analysis of his financial behavior.

As Joel struggles to change Janet's attitude toward him in their life together, a parallel struggle is occurring inside him. One part of his personality — which for present purposes I'll call his inner female — mistrusts another part — his inner male. In other words, as if Janet's criticism were not enough, Joel has *self-doubts* about his financial responsibility.

Even though he is not conscious of doubting himself in this way, such feelings affect Joel's state of mind nonetheless, especially when Janet begins to criticize him. Whenever she even intimates that she is concerned about their money situation, this sets off in Joel reverberations of inner conflict. He tries to silence her doubts in an effort to silence his own. But Janet refuses to be silenced. She senses Joel's inner struggle, and it only exacerbates her fears. Janet continues to express her doubts; Joel becomes more and more angry and resentful. And eventually the two decide to divorce.

In a year, Joel remarries. For a while Joel and his new wife Sara seem totally compatible, with no reason for struggle or conflict. Another year goes by, and Sara, too, begins to doubt Joel's sense of financial responsibility. Joel, again feeling misunderstood and uncared for, leaves Sara for Leslie, who appears quite an opposite type from both Janet and Sara. Leslie is carefree, lighthearted and seems to have nothing to worry about. Joel now feels assured that he will not have to deal with another doubting woman!

But this time, something unexpected occurs: instead of Leslie criticizing Joel's financial irresponsibility, he finds himself being annoyed by hers! Leslie can't hold a job. She is continually bouncing checks. And Joel fears she will become totally dependent on him financially. He now gets a chance to experience the "other side of the coin."

By now an inner light of awareness is beginning to dawn in Joel. He starts to wonder if perhaps he hasn't been looking in the wrong direction in his efforts to resolve this struggle over financial responsibility. Maybe instead of attempting to find ever-more-compatible mates, he needs to look at his relationship to himself — at the relationship between his own inner male and female.

Maybe the recurring struggle in relationship to Janet, Sara, and Leslie is simply a mirror of Joel's inner conflict. And maybe such an awareness can lead to a change in this frustrating pattern.

As Joel is able to acknowledge his self-doubts, he no longer needs to attract women who do his doubting for him. Nor need he find the opposite type of woman on whom to project his inner doubts. As he recognizes and accepts his own concern for his doubtful financial competence, the women in his life no longer need to take care of this for him. They become "miraculously" less concerned with this area of life, trusting Joel to deal with himself in these matters. Thus,

Joel's interpersonal struggle over financial responsibility disappears as he stops projecting his inner struggle outward.

Many people discover recurring themes and patterns in their relationship lives, as Joel did. A woman notices that she seems repeatedly to be attracted to unavailable men. Or perhaps a man finds that people both at home and at work are always trying to get him to slow down. Often a particular pattern will remain dominant for a period of years until some significant crisis occurs and leads to the resolution of the pattern. Then, it is usually only a matter of time before another pattern, representing another rung on the ladder of growth, emerges to be dealt with.

## Physical Violence Against One's Other Side

A few years ago an example of how the outer relationship reflects the inner came to national attention via the news media. A famous professional football player was repeatedly arrested for physically assaulting the women he dated. He was always attracted to very petite, helpless, frail women — women who seemed to be opposite in type from himself. He was initially attracted to these women "for unexplainable reasons," he disclosed. But after a short while, "their weakness made me sick."

I knew this man personally and could see why his attraction soon turned to repulsion. A man who worked constantly at appearing tough, strong, even invincible, he vigorously denied the softer, "weaker" side of himself. He couldn't stand to get too close to those qualities in others, lest he be reminded of his own soft side. While the masculine side of his personality had been dominant, the feminine side exerted an unconscious force, as revealed in his attraction to softness. When he became aware of his own soft and tender feelings in relation to a woman, a violent unconscious reaction was stirred in him. He wanted to destroy the source of his uncomfortable feelings. Thus, his attacks on women.

If this "macho man" could have allowed expression to his softer side instead of projecting it outward, he could have accepted softness in others without feeling threatened. In other words, if he could have developed a more harmonious relationship between his inner masculine and inner feminine aspects, he would have had more harmonious relationships with females.

I did not personally know any of the women he dated, but I assume that their attraction to this big strong football hero was no accident. I imagine that they were in some way out of touch with their inner power, perhaps even frightened of it. Thus, they found themselves in a relationship with someone whose strength scared them.

In relationships where attraction and repulsion seem to ebb and flow rapidly, it is probable that the phenomenon described here is at work. A love/hate relationship with another mirrors a love/hate relationship within oneself. While there may also be other factors involved, a good starting point for resolving such a power struggle is to search for the power struggle within.

## Balancing Power and Love

The process of balancing the inner masculine and the inner feminine can be a lifelong affair. The traits and feelings which make up these two sides of the human persona are extremely complex and often contradictory.

For some men and women, the inner male is a symbol for such qualities as power, strength, and daring. For others, their inner male is associated with achievements in the domains of logic and mental activity. For still others, especially females who already feel powerful and achieving, the inner male may be symbolic of a relaxed, wise, spiritual inner presence.

Likewise, the symbolic inner female of either men or women can be soft and tender, emotional and provocative, or comforting and wise.

The task of a lifetime is to bring these inner polarities into consciousness and harmony. The job is accomplished through one's relationships with others. In some relationships this process is long and difficult. In others it is played out quite succinctly.

Matthew and Vicki, a couple in their early thirties, have been living together for two years. They hope one day to be married, but there are problems they want to resolve before they make a lifelong commitment to each other. Matthew is a tall, slender man, almost willowy. His movements are graceful and flowing, his manner gentle. Vicki is a solidly-built, attractive brunette with an abundance of vigor and vitality. She maintains a year-round suntan, which along with her sleek muscular body gives her the appearance of a lifeguard or a surfer.

In their relationship, Vicki is the powerful, competent one, and Matthew is the loving, easy-going one. Before meeting Matthew, Vicki had already noticed a pattern in her attractions to men: she always fell in love with men she saw as more receptive, more yielding than herself. As a result, it often felt to her as if she were playing the "masculine" role in the relationship. Not surprisingly, this caused conflict with her partners. Both had been socialized to expect the traditional role division between women and men. What's more, Vicki herself could not accept what she considered to be an imbalance between her masculine and feminine sides. She felt she should be more feminine and that her man should be more masculine, which to her meant more active, more able to take charge.

Thus, Vicki and her partners found themselves in frequent power struggles around the question of who would initiate or *send* in the relationship, and who would respond or *receive*. Vicki wanted to receive more, but because of the type of men she attracted, this seemed impossible. She hadn't developed within herself sufficient trust and comfort with the receptive aspect of her nature. She had a hard time, for example, waiting for a man to approach her at a social gathering. She found herself compelled to make the first approach. As a result, she usually found herself with men who were receptive and approachable, but who were not able to

make the first move toward her because they had not
developed their more active sides. Thus, Vicki gave herself
little opportunity to receive.

Matthew, of course, had an opposite and complementary
pattern. He had always been attracted to women who were
capable and strong, qualities he would like to have had in his
own personality. But since he was not truly comfortable with
these qualities in himself, he often found himself arguing with
women about their excessive needs for power and control.

When Vicki and Matthew met, both had a history of
many short-lived and conflict-filled relationships. They had
given up on intimacy more than once because "the kind of
person I'm attracted to is a type I can't get along with." Both
being former students of psychology and human behavior,
they had some insight into their hopelessness. They saw their
lack of inner balance as the cause for their dissatisfaction with
potential partners. But this insight did not move them an inch
further toward heterosexual harmony. Each often blamed the
other for their problem. Vicki felt that if only Matthew could
be more masculine, she would be able to be more feminine.
Likewise, Matthew accused Vicki of being so over-active that
it left him no room to take the initiative she so desired of him.

Sometime during this power struggle, each of them
unexpectedly gave in, surrendering to their own inner states
of imbalance. They decided to stop fighting it and learn to
accept it. Vicki stopped demanding perfection from herself.
Matthew got sick and tired of always trying to make himself
over. They both, almost simultaneously, saw their struggle as
an unrealistic quest for an ideal state of balance. Very few
people *ever* attain such balance; Vicki and Matthew realized
and accepted that they were not going to achieve it quickly.
They recognized it as a lifelong learning process, and saw that
they could help and teach each other if they could show a little
more patience.

Accepting their inner imbalance and the pain it had
brought them allowed them to relax into a posture of
openness to learning from each other. This led Vicki to change

her way of asking for what she wanted from Matthew. Instead of insisting that he should express himself more powerfully, she asked Matthew to try to approach her more often in order to help her learn to be comfortable receiving. In other words, she asked for his help instead of demanding that he improve. This, of course, was much easier for Matthew to hear sympathetically, since he now felt her need, rather than her criticism and impatience with him.

Matthew asked Vicki to acknowledge and support his efforts to show more initiative, to warmly receive his gestures toward her — again as a way of helping *him*, not of improving herself.

Matthew and Vicki had understood all along how their inner conflicts tended to get replayed in their outer life, but this insight was only the first step. The quantum leap toward harmony occurred when each could *stop fighting and accept* the inner conflict. They may not have liked it, but fighting it was not the answer. Self-acceptance grew from their willingness to let go, and brought them to a new way of asking for what they wanted from each other. They became able to acknowledge their inner imbalance to each other, and with this acknowledgement came a great relief. They no longer needed to mask their own inadequacies, and could simply ask each other for help when it was needed.

## The Bulldog at my Door

When I look at the course of my own love life, I can see many examples of how my relationship to myself is reflected in my relationships with men.

I think it was during my late teens that I first became aware of a recurring pattern in my relationships. I noticed that I always attracted and was attracted to possessive, rather overprotective men. They used to snarl, show their teeth, and flex their muscles whenever other men would come around me. Even though I liked the men I was involved with, I didn't like their territorial behavior. I felt as if a big bulldog kept watch at the door of my house, barking at all potential intruders. When I would express this to them, they would tell me that I was too open and too trusting, and they feared that I would let people into my house who didn't belong just because I didn't want to be mean to anyone.

It took several years of living out this pattern with men before I recognized it. These bulldogs had my number all along, and I didn't know it. I was just a girl who couldn't say no! I let them say my no's for me. That way, I was able to maintain a self-image of openness and generosity: "I'd really love to spend more time with you, but my boyfriend wouldn't like it."

Once I recognized the pattern, I realized how I had denied expression of my own bulldog capacities, allowing others to play this role in my life and then criticizing them for it! As my awareness of myself expanded to include the ability to say no as well as yes, I stopped attracting bulldogs to me. …Or did the men in my life simply stop *acting* like bulldogs?

## The Disowned Inner Critic

The next pattern I encountered was my repeated attraction to hypercritical men who seemed to feel it their duty to point out my foibles and shortcomings. This pattern caused me considerable pain and confusion, as I wondered: "I have relatively high self-esteem. Why do I choose such nit-pickers?!" Again, as I looked more carefully into my situation, I realized that I was almost never critical of myself. I could overlook the most glaring incompetencies and inconsistencies — as long as they were my own! As a consequence, those close to me felt called upon to help me see the things about myself that I tended to deny: my limitations and shortcomings.

Learning to be realistically self-critical was a gradual process for me. At first, I had to become less fearful of criticism from others. Eventually I could feel relaxed enough in the presence of negative feedback to confront my own inner critic. As I came to accept this inner critic as a valuable and useful part of myself, the men in my life became "miraculously" uncritical.

It can be said, with only slight oversimplification, that *we get into power struggles with others to the extent that our own inner parts are in conflict with each other.*

In the case of my own inner critic, for example, we can assume that I had the *potential* for realistic self-criticism within me all along, but some part of me, perhaps the "hypersensitive little girl," did not want to hear from the critical part. She would rather not have known important things about herself than feel the pain of criticism. After awareness of my denial became unavoidable, however, the sensitive little girl slowly opened up to the critic.

Open communication among one's inner aspects is the way to peaceful coexistence and inner harmony. Open inner dialogue brings about an exchange of perspectives between the various impulses within one's psyche. This allows one's various subpersonalities to have a moderating influence on one another. Your various inner voices are actually talking sympathetically with one another instead of trying to dominate or ignore each other.

Such inner dialogue keeps us out of the trap of overidentification with one aspect of the self to the exclusion of other aspects. Thus, a desire to achieve and a desire for relaxation moderate and blend with one another to prevent both hyperactivity and lethargy, to allow an easy but energetic movement through the world. When you are in such a state of inner harmony, you attract relationships that are harmonious, because you do not need others to help fight your inner battles.

Harmony is relative, however, since most of us are in a process of becoming more and more self-aware. Thus, as we attain harmony in one sphere of life, we often find a new, perhaps even more elusive, inner struggle emerging to take its place.

The path to wholeness and harmony may not get easier, but it does begin to make more sense after a while!

## The Price Per Pound Theory

A friend of mine has a theory about sexual attraction, which he calls "the price per pound theory." It goes something like this: hamburger attracts hamburger, steak attracts steak, lobster attracts lobster. Each cut of meat, so to speak, has a different "price per pound." And even though it is true that opposites attract in terms of personal style, the price per pound theory holds that one tends to be attracted to someone who is at a similar level of integration, inner harmony or consciousness. Thus, people who are just beginning to awaken to the natural growth process of which all life partakes, will attract others at a similar stage of personal development. People who have been working toward self-realization for a while will prefer to be in the company of others with comparable experience.

It is as if each particular "cut" — or level of inner harmony and openness — vibrates at its own frequency, and resonates most naturally with other beings on the same frequency. Acceptance of and relaxation with one's own frequency leads to satisfaction with those who are attracted to it. When we resist acknowledging our current level of personal development, we will tend to be dissatisfied with what life deals to us. We find ourselves struggling to hold on to relationships that are inappropriate and unsatisfying. I am reminded of the famous protest of Groucho Marx (and later Woody Allen): 'I wouldn't want to belong to any club that would accept me as a member!'' Allen, our culture's caricatured hero of low self-esteem, cannot be satisfied with anyone who would be fool enough to be satisfied with him.

You've probably heard the remark: "The people who are attracted to me just don't interest me." What is really going on here? What are these people saying about themselves? According to the price per pound theory, these people either cannot recognize or cannot accept their current price per pound or level of inner realization. The secret to inner happiness or relationship satisfaction is in loving and accepting yourself for where you are, not in holding grand aspirations. You only attain your next level or lesson on the self-realization journey when you fully accept where you are.

In the game of man-woman attraction, it is impossible to fool another person for very long. *Trying* to attract a certain kind of partner will lead to a constantly painful relationship, one in which you can never relax and be yourself, where you feel always on guard or on edge, unconsciously fearful of being found out or losing the other person's love. Your true state can be seen and felt by others no matter how skillfully you may camouflage it!

How many times have you felt afraid of being seen as you are, in either a love or a work relationship? A fear that if the other person *really* knew you, he would not accept you. And how many times, as a consequence, have you found yourself hiding and feeling vaguely anxious about it? This internal state of uneasiness is evidence of the fact that you need to surrender your false self-image and trade it in for a more compassionately realistic one.

If you can love yourself as you are, you will attract the love of others, even if you are 4'1'' and weigh 300 pounds. If you let yourself be dominated by your pride and arrogance, which often come disguised as extreme self-criticism and judgmentalness toward others, you will find yourself continually in relationships with people you feel aren't good enough for you. You will find yourself criticizing them for not living up to your ideal, when actually this is an impossible demand. You will not be able to appreciate the positive qualities they do have, since your attention is always focused on what is missing.

All this criticalness stems from your own lack of self-acceptance. When you recognize that there are valid reasons why you attract the people you do, then you will be able to learn and grow in all your relationships.

The price per pound theory is not a "law of nature," however, most growth facilitators — teachers, psychologists, therapists, coaches — find that we learn life's lessons best in the company of people who are just slightly more aware and integrated than ourselves. A paradox. So how can we create relationships for ourselves that show us the way while at the same time respecting the notion that the best mates are of approximately the same cut?

The resolution of this paradox lies, I believe, in recognizing that many of our most significant love and work relationships are primarily for the purpose of *learning lessons*, and not for the purpose of becoming *mates*, where partners actually create something together beyond the relationship. Some relationships have both a learning and a creative purpose, but many do not. It is better to accept these learning relationships for what they are, rather than trying to force-fit them into the mating mold.

Trying to make your relationship conform to an ideal image can only lead to needless struggle. Of course, the sooner two learning partners accept the status of their bond and get on with learning what they have come to teach each other, the sooner they can transform their relationship into a creative one, or move on to a more suitable mate.

The mating dance, or courtship period, is a time for sensing each other's vibrational (price per pound) compatibility. If a harmonious resonance occurs and persists over time, partners know they are mates, meant to create out of their individuality and their separateness a third entity (material or spiritual) which expresses their unity. If a dissonance persists during the mating dance, partners would be well-advised to accept the learner status of their bond, instead of continually comparing their relationship to a fantasized ideal.

Many spiritual traditions recommend that young people develop loving non-sexual relationships with persons more experienced in life in order to learn certain relationship lessons, such as how to say no gracefully, or how to offer loving criticism, without unnecessary pain and disappointment. This is the concept of the mentor. You can have mentors in both love and work — people who consciously reflect to you a higher possibility within yourself. A mentor relationship is different from a mate relationship, although both involve mutual influence and learning. When mentor and mentee are also lovers, however, it is best not to pretend or wish to be mates, as this only causes unnecessary suffering.

Power struggles often occur where partners in a mentor-mentee relationship try to make the relationship into something that cannot be, for the time being at least. Unconsciously, the mentor may try to get the partner to hurry up, to develop more quickly. Or the mentee may envy or resent the mentor for having the very qualities she seeks to learn about. If the two could simply recognize that they are of different prices per pound, they could relax and enjoy the relationship for what it is.

The price per pound theory does not imply that mate relationships are without conflict or struggle. What it does emphasize, however, is that some partners are naturally resonant and others are more dissonant. Think of the couples you know. Some look and feel as if they belong together even if they have many superficial dissimilarities, such as culture, age and professional background. They radiate compatibility in spite of their outer differences. With other couples, you wonder how these two ever make it together. You can feel the disharmony between them. It obviously takes great effort for them to sustain their bond.

This statement is not meant to downgrade the less harmonious, learning-oriented unions. It is rather my way of calling attention to the fact that there are things that we perceive about our own and others' relationships that we may prefer not to admit that we see. Somehow we seem loathe to admit not only our own inner conflicts and relationship problems, but also our perception of these in other people. It is as if we have made a silent pact with others to ignore what we see and feel and instead believe what they tell us.

If we could all more easily acknowledge to each other our true, though perhaps disquieting, observations, we would

have a better chance of helping each other learn and develop
more satisfying relationships. We need to take our differences
and difficulties less seriously so that we can face them more
honestly.

Price per pound differences with the man or woman of
your fantasies need not be catastrophic. To love a person who
can only be your mentor, never your mate, does not mean that
the entire relationship is doomed. Although it seems
paradoxical, we are more likely to do something about our
difficulties when we treat them with a certain lightness of
spirit, a certain humility. Unrealistic expectations and
idealized images can only lead to struggle.

**ten:** Sex: Changing Expectations, Unchanging Biology

Sexuality is probably the most sensitive yet misunderstood area of interpersonal relationships. Nowhere else do our conflicts and hangups reveal themselves quite so blatantly or so painfully. Through sexual intimacy we seek validation of our lovability; yet we often find that differences in sexual appetite or rhythm make this quest extremely difficult.

In the workplace also it is important to bring our sexual selves into the picture, in pursuit not of sex but of wholeness. If we try to exorcise our maleness or femaleness from our work personas, we lose a certain vitality and power — a power which can contribute much to success on the job.

Whether in love or at work, sex is both a great mystery and a great necessity. And, with the rapidly changing sexual mores and role expectations of men and women, our confusion intensifies. It used to be that men were the initiators of sexual encounters, and women the receivers or rejectors. Now, women are almost as likely as men to initiate, and to be received or rejected.

We used to think women were all interested in marriage and long-term commitments, while men were expected to resist being snared, or at least pretend to resist. Nowadays

among my single acquaintances, I meet more men than
women who are seeking a long-term committed relationship.
How often have I heard these men complain, ''I'm looking for
a mate for life, but all the women I meet are putting their
careers first and marriage second!''

From single women the reply goes something like this,
''Sure, I'm interested in marriage, but I want to establish
myself in my career first...I'm not willing to be emotionally or
financially dependent on a man. I need a life independent
from my role as wife.'' Such a change is bound to affect the
way men and women relate together in bed.

Another change which seems to be wreaking havoc with
sexual relationships is the attempt by both men and women to
become more conscious, more androgynous, more evolved.
Any of these or similar aims tend to cause people to think
more about their relationships than they used to, for better or
for worse. Sometimes when people *think* a lot about how they
want to be, instead of *accepting* how they are, their
interactions lose spontaneity. I've noticed this phenomenon
especially among poeple who are working toward becoming
less emotional, less egocentric, more ''transpersonal.'' These
people often complain (or their partners complain for them)
that their sex life has lost its fire. They no longer feel the
sexual passion or hunger they once felt. They have become so
dis-identified with their sexual feeling as to approach
detachment. Perhaps as people are becoming less instinctual
in their sexuality, they are also becoming less sexy.

The attempt to become androgynous — to blend male
and female roles — has apparently also led to a gap between
people's ideals and their actual behavior. It is a familiar
refrain nowadays from non-sexist, liberated males that,
''Women say they want men to be more sensitive and gentle,
but when it comes right down to choosing a mate, they still
seem to go for the macho types.''

Likewise, how often I have heard the other side of this
story from my women friends, ''Men say they like women who
have developed their talents and abilities and their

individuality, but they seem to really prefer the ones who are beautiful, sexy and focused on pleasing a man, regardless of her other qualities.''

The sexual climate of the times is obviously changing. Yet there are certain things about males' and females' sexual natures that perhaps change only very slowly if they change at all. By accepting these less malleable aspects of our natures, perhaps we can approach the question of male-female sexuality with more understanding.

## Sexual Differences Between Males and Females

If the changing social expectations for sexuality are creating confusion, the unchanging biological and socio-biological differences may seem utterly mystifying! Our faith in Nature's wisdom in putting everything in the right places breaks down when we begin to consider other ''facts of life'':

— Males apparently reach the peak of their need for sexual release around the age of 19 or 20; females' sexual interest gradually increases to its peak in the late 30's. What Nature had in mind when she created this apparent sexual discontinuity, we'll never know! What it tends to create, however, is sexual mismatches among mates of the same age. Now, I'm not saying that this is a bad thing. It is simply a problem to be solved, and one which may lead to a power struggle as each person tries to mold the couple's sex life to suit his or her needs.

Problems and power struggles can be avenues to deeper understanding. Such struggle can cause partners to stretch themselves in the direction of the loved-one's wishes, possibly overcoming a bit of ego-centeredness in the process. Perhaps this is what Nature had in mind after all!

— The story of male and female sexual development over the lifespan is mirrored in each single sexual enounter: not only do men reach their sexual peak earlier in life, men also tend to warm up in any single lovemaking session more quickly than do women. What this accomplishes once again is an opportunity for the man and woman to work out a way of dealing with this difference.

If the man naturally warms up faster and comes more quickly, the situation calls for him to go against this instinctive tendency (that is, to overcome his self-centered urge) if his pleasure is to be shared by his partner. The woman, on the other hand, must take the risk of letting her man know what pleases her. This requires that she be more trusting and vulnerable and less self-protective than she might otherwise be.

— The man's primary sex organs are located outside of his body, in plain view; the woman's are internal and out of sight. This tends to put the man in a more vulnerable position, since he cannot so easily hide his feelings of attraction or pretend to be aroused when he is not. This is another inequality between the sexes which can lead to a lack of empathy or understanding of each other's positions. Each may think the other has an easier time with the difficult and tender matter of sexual arousal.

— And now we come to the potentially most volatile of all differences. Research evidence from the field of sociobiology suggests that there may be an instinctual tendency for males to be polygamous while females are monogamous. In all animals which reproduce via sexual intercourse, the male's fulfillment of his role in species propagation calls upon him to find as many willing females as possible to receive his sperm. This is due in part to the fact that many millions of sperm are sent forth but few are chosen in Nature's egg-sperm fertility dance. Thus, the more sent forth — into the greatest number of potential recipients — the greater the chance that this male will successfully fulfill his biological reproductive role.

For the female of any species, because of her very different reproductive role, the situation is reversed. It is in her interest to hold to her the one male who fertilizes her once-a-month (in the case of humans) ovum. To fulfill her biological destiny, she must undergo a delicate gestation period during which she is somewhat dependent on a constant mate to provide her with food, shelter, protection or other assistance.

Thus, for the male animal, his role in species survival can occur without ever bonding with a permanent mate. For the female, fertilization of her egg is only the beginning. The main part of her role occurs in the gestation and care of her young, during which time it behooves her to attract a faithful mate.

Obviously there is a lot more to human sexuality than reproduction. And we may hope there is a lot more than our animal heritage motivating us. However, given the recurring battles between men and women over the monogamy-nonmonogamy issue, one wonders about the roots of this conflict.

Was it man, woman, or beast who composed the familiar, ''Higamous, hogamous, women are monogamous. Hogamous, higamous, men are polygamous''?

— Related to this sociobiological analysis is another dealing with the male animal's purported greater need for sexual variety. The research here bears reporting, though it is scanty and comes from studies in the breeding of farm animals, especially cattle. Farmers have noticed that a bull when put to mate with a cow will soon grow fatigued and stop what he is doing; the female shows no such signs of fatigue. However, if at that moment another, new and different, cow is brought in for the same bull to mate, he will pursue the engagement with renewed vigor.

Now, there's a great gap between bull consciousness and human consciousness, but I'll wager that many of my readers, both male and female, are recognizing in these animal stories themselves or someone they love.

The major implication of all these sociobiological differences is that partners need to make adjustments to each other's rhythms, moods and preferences. To achieve harmony, compromise is necessary. In a close relationship the fact of interdependence becomes inescapable. If your partner does not enjoy sex, you will not enjoy it fully either. Thus, you are motivated to pay attention to the others' needs as well as your own. This brings an expanded quality of consciousness to your actions. Your identity as a self grows beyond the bounds of your own ''skin-encapsulated ego,'' as Alan Watts used to say. You come to feel energetically one with your partner, resulting in a subtle but profound refinement of your sexual responsiveness. When this occurs, compromise is no longer necessary.

This process of growth through harmonizing differences is what the couple's journey is about. In sex the process simply becomes accelerated and magnified. In the next section, I will discuss some things that a couple can do intentionally to help the process along.

## The Meaning of Impotence and Frigidity

Many men and women go through one or more phases in their lives during which they are unable to enjoy sex. How each partner interprets this unwelcome occurrence will determine whether or not it leads to struggle.

Herb and Wanda had enjoyed a compatible sexual relationship for nearly fifteen years when Herb suddenly became impotent. At first Wanda felt hurt and rejected. She suspected that he was losing interest in her and that he was perhaps seeing someone else. She told him about her feelings, and asked for his explanation. Herb was as upset and bewildered as she, and could not give her a reason because he did not understand it himself. He reassured Wanda of his love for her, and confided his own worry about his condition.

Once reassured, Wanda became quite patient with Herb's difficulty. She found many new ways for them to share physical pleasure without requiring that he have an erection. Herb was especially appreciative of her leadership at this critical time, because he was too unsure of himself to take much sexual initiative.

Wanda's attitude in this situation is an expression of the Unity/Participation attitude described in Chapter Eight. She was able to love what she had, rather than worrying about what she was missing.

After a few months, Herb regained his normal sexual response. The crisis had a beneficial effect upon their relationship. During the months they were deprived of their usual sexual fare, they had expanded the variety of ways for expressing their love.

Herb's and Wanda's crisis might have led to a different outcome if either or both had given a different meaning to the situation. What if Wanda had been unable to let go of her suspicions about Herb? What if Herb had seen his temporary impotence as such a threat to his manhood that he avoided sex entirely? The meanings we attach to the events that occur in our lives make all the difference in determining whether a crisis will lead to deepening or destruction of a relationship.

There are times, however, when it is appropriate to seek a less benign motive for a symptom like impotence or frigidity. Often a person will lose sexual responsiveness toward a partner because of anger, disappointment or resentment.

Lynn and Robbie had been together for nine years when their crisis occurred. Lynn could no longer respond to Robbie's advances. Knowing Robbie well, Lynn suspected jealous anger at the obvious interest Lynn had shown toward a mutual friend. Robbie, however, denied any anger or jealousy, claimed to love Lynn as much as ever, and insisted that all that was needed was time and patience. Lynn did not buy it; Robbie was obviously hiding some strong feelings. Nevertheless, Lynn's best efforts failed to draw them out.

Instead of continuing to be nice and patient with Robbie, Lynn finally blew up, expressing hurt and resentment about being sexually exploited. Careful to take responsibility for the anger and hurt feelings, Lynn told Robbie how the apparent deception was hurting the relationship, but did not blame or accuse Robbie of intentional or spiteful behavior. Lynn's angry blow-up gave Robbie a chance to become angry in return, and many months of buried resentments were hurled in both directions.

In the heat of this battle, Robbie admitted being angry at Lynn's lack of caring and respect, shown particularly by flirtatious behavior in public. Following this fiery exchange, Lynn and Robbie found their caring for one another was rekindled, sexually and otherwise. Robbie thanked Lynn for pushing them to the much-needed confrontation, and for the improved communication which resulted.

## Varieties of Sexual Scripts

Power struggles often occur when you suspect that your partner holds a different attitude about sex than you do. One reason that the area of sexuality is associated with so much tension is that sex means such different things to each of us. To one person, the act of lovemaking signifies a sacred and inviolate bond; to another it is simply a momentary pleasure soon to be forgotten. Some people are at their best when they are free to roam from one sexual encounter to another; others are happiest when strongly and permanently bonded to one partner.

Upbringing and cultural expectations often lead people to behave as if they felt one way about sex when in actuality they feel quite the opposite. A woman who has been taught that sexual intercourse signifies love and commitment may find herself extremely confused after having a light-hearted temporary affair. Her self-picture does not permit such indulgences, and yet she has just violated this self-picture with no apparent negative consequences.

A person may hold beliefs which give sex too much importance or too little. Some struggle can be expected when a husband holds the sexual part of a marriage sacred and inviolate and his wife does not. Some people have difficulty limiting their sexual expression to one partner out of a fear of becoming too dependent on that person. Others like to stay

free of sexual commitments because they derive a feeling of
power from sexual conquest or from being needed by their
partners. Still others, as with Bart and Betty in chapter Seven,
feel they need a degree of sexual variety in order to maintain
their sense of vitality and aliveness.

All of these styles and preferences are based on self
images or belief systems. Who you are is who you tell yourself
you are, for practical purposes anyway.

Persons with conflicting sexual scripts or self-pictures
may be attracted to one another because each — consciously
or not — wants to learn more about his or her own sexuality.
A conflict *between* two people almost invariably mirrors a
conflict already in progress *within* each of them. In sex,
perhaps more than in any other area of potential conflict, a
struggle occurring between you and another person is a signal
that there is also a part of yourself struggling to be
acknowledged or expressed.

## Ways of Harmonizing Sexual Differences
— *Talking*

The most important method for harmonizing sexual
differences is straightforward, loving, verbal communication.
Simply telling each other how you're feeling, what gives you
pleasure and what makes you uncomfortable — these are the
things that can make or break a couple's sex life. Many people
don't like to talk about sex. They either feel that it's too
sacred for discussion or that good sex should come naturally,
without being explicit about it.

The truth is that sexual harmony does not occur naturally
for most couples. All the interpersonal differences I've
discussed throughout the book come strongly into play in the
sexual part of a relationship. You cannot assume that what
pleases you will please your partner or that what you like to
give is what he or she likes to receive. Loving someone well
means giving what that someone needs to receive, not what
you need to give. And this requires knowing and accepting
your partner's other-ness. Your partner is not your clone,
even though you may wish at times for more similarity.

If you accept your differences as normal and natural, sex can be a delightful and enlightening harmonizing force in your lives. If you resist your differences, thinking or wishing it should all be more spontaneous, sex can be pretty stressful.

Another deterrent to open communication about sex is shame. Shame is really a type of fear, fear that something about one's sexuality is unwholesome or unacceptable, accompanied by a fear of being seen or exposed. Many people have sexual fantasies, preferences or fetishes which originated early in childhood before they adopted society's conventions of appropriateness. As a result, some of the things that feel good to them are unique only to them; and they fear this is somehow not normal.

Perhaps, for example, some way your mother used to touch you when she changed your diapers has remained with you until this day in your repertoire of sexual preferences. But you may have no idea where it originated, and from talking to friends, you know this preference is not shared by others. So you try to hide from your sexual partner some information about yourself that could offer you much pleasure. You may hope he or she will accidentally discover your secret pleasure area, but otherwise you would rather sacrifice feeling good in favor of looking good. In time you may even come to resent your partner's insensitivity for not discovering your secret.

Your partner may intuit that you have distanced yourself sexually, but will probably never dream of the reason. (You may not even be conscious of it yourself.) If both of you are too shy, fearful or lazy to mention this distancing that has occurred, it will probably continue and may even reverberate to other areas of your relationship. If one of you does mention it, you now have the opportunity to make amends. Chances are, if you take a risk and 'fess up, your partner will feel closer to you for the trust you have shown. Chances are also that your disclosure will help pave the way for similar openness on your partner's part. Usually people need to feel a sense of caring, trust and permission before opening up their hidden areas. Your confession provides permission for your partner.

You are in effect saying, "I can accept you with all your 'deviations,' since I accept my own."

Many people avoid verbalizing about sex because they feel it is so sacred or so profound that words cannot do justice to their feelings. I respect this objection. Yet I also feel that sometimes it is the very fact that the feelings seem beyond words that makes expression so important. To attempt to communicate a profound or tender feeling to one's partner is a gesture of great caring. You are taking a risk, making yourself more open and vulnerable. Even when the verbal expression falls far short of the inner feeling, your partner will probably appreciate your attempt to deepen the level of communication between you.

— *Breathing Together*

An obvious, but often overlooked, indicator of two people's differing rhythms is shown in their breathing. Some people breathe slowly and deeply. Others breathe more quickly and shallowly. Your breathing pulse is part of your character to some degree, but it also reflects your state of tension or relaxation. If two people can learn to synchronize their breathing while lying together (side by side or holding one another, eyes closed), they are well on their way to synchronizing other physical rhythms.

Learning to synchronize your breathing involves attuning yourself to the other's subtle energy flow. As you pay careful attention to your own and your partner's breathing at the same time, you are developing your ability to hold in your attention *both* states of being. You are learning not to be distracted from your own feelings by attending to your partner. And at the same time you are learning not to allow your own feelings and impulses to totally dominate your attention.

Lying down and breathing together is a relaxing, meditative way to spend time together. There are no expectations involved aside from quietly paying attention to both breathing patterns. This is not intended as a prelude to sex, although if that occurs spontaneously, it's fine.

I have known couples who practice this ritual as a regular way of tuning up their relationship. When they feel themselves getting out of touch with the subtler dimensions of being together, they call for a time of breathing together.

## — Looking

When you see deeply into another person, you allow yourself to come under the influence of that person. At the same time, you increase your influence upon the other.

Christ said, "The eye is the lamp of the body." Through it you receive the key ingredient of enlightenment — light. It is also said that the eyes are like windows to the soul. If you let others look into these windows, they will be able to see the essence that is you, beneath the persona which you ordinarily wear.

Looking into each other's eyes is a meditative ritual similar to breathing together. It is harder to maintain your focus of attention in this as compared with the breathing exercise because the eyes are open. Open eyes allow into the mind all kinds of distractions along with the light they receive. My experience tells me that it's usually best to engage in this exercise only after you have had considerable practice with the breathing exercise.

To perform the looking ritual, sit facing your partner, close enough so you can see his/her eyes without straining. Then focus a relaxed gaze toward your partner's left eye, and just sit there looking into one another. Breathe slowly and deeply, but don't worry about whether your breathing is synchronized. Allow yourself to blink whenever it feels natural. This is not a staring contest. Now, stay together this way for five to fifteen minutes.

We choose the left eye to focus on because the left eye carries impulses to and from the right hemisphere of the brain, the hemisphere which is thought to be less used in normal thinking activities. Thus, we are giving a little more

energy to a part of ourselves that gets less attention in this
culture, and therefore is perhaps less acculturated and more
open.

Couples who practice this looking exercise report that it
helps them to become less shy with each other, sexually and
otherwise. It also seems to act as a vehicle for deepening
acceptance of one another, which in turn helps in becoming
more accommodating to each other's rhythms and
preferences.

— *Balancing Roles*

Often couples find after a time of being together sexually
that they have gotten into a rut, an inflexible pattern of always
doing things the same way. Perhaps he is always the one who
initiates their sexual encounters. Or perhaps she is always the
one who talks about sex, while he is habitually silent. If,
reflecting upon your relationship, you discover yourselves to
be in such a rut, you may want to try this balancing ritual for
an agreed-upon period of time.

The ritual involves, first of all, identifying the pattern you
seem to be in, noting particularly any fixed roles you have
each assumed. (See Chapter Three for assistance in
identifying your patterns.) Then decide together what the
reverse of this role would be for each of you. For example, if
his role is as initiator, the reverse of this might be responder.
Or if her role is usually talker, the reverse might be to be
silent in order to leave space for him to talk. Once you decide
on the reverse of your usual role, spend some time forming a
clear mental image of how you would behave in this new role.
Then, go ahead and try it in a spirit of playful
experimentation.

There is no right way for the experiment to turn out. The
aim is not to be successful in reversing your roles. It is more a
question of using this ritual and the decision to try a new
behavior as a way of helping you see yourself and your
partner more clearly. You may notice, for example, if you are
a talker, that after a few days you begin to despair about the

silence all around you. Your partner has not (yet?) come in to fill the space that you've left. You get anxious and declare the experiment a failure. I want to emphasize that there is no failure in this ritual. What you learn about yourself and your partner is important information. It can help you to accept things as they are and accommodate to them rather than always wishing things were different.

So please, don't think you know how the experiment should turn out. Enter it in the spirit of a true researcher, a true self-scientist. And remember, your aim is information about yourselves, not a change in your pattern.

— *Sex Without Orgasm*

Many women practice sex without orgasm regularly. Generally this is not out of choice. It occurs because of many of the male-female sex differences we've already discussed, and also because most women are socialized to be givers of nurturance more than receivers.

Most men, on the other hand, experience some kind of orgasm, although the quality may vary greatly, every time they make love. Only a minority of men have learned the alternative pleasure of voluntarily abstaining from orgasm. Such voluntary abstention may, for example, allow him to maintain a feeling of heightened sexual energy in a way that enhances his sense of well-being for an extended period of time. Or it may alter his focus of attention during sex so that he now derives as much pleasure from his partner's response as from his own.

In order for a woman to learn the alternative pleasures of such voluntary abstention, she will generally need to have a partner who is also abstaining. This sets the mood of lovemaking toward mutual exploration and pleasuring, rather than on the goal of orgasm. It allows a woman whose orgastic response may be somewhat temperamental to play around with those feelings in herself which lead to orgasm, without becoming distracted by her partner's intensity or by the presence of a goal. Sex without orgasm is really goal-less sex.

It can therefore be, for some people, more open, exploratory and relaxed.

The nice thing about it, for couples who have difficulty synchronizing their sexual response cycles, is that a shared experience is insured. Both partners experience heightened sexual feeling together without release.

To practice this rather disciplined ritual, it is necessary first to agree, in an attitude of open experimentation, that you'd both like to try it. Then decide on a period of time. Most couples start with two weeks to a month. After that they go back to normal sex, finding that the period of "celibacy" has changed their lovemaking pattern in some way. Some couples use this practice about once a year as a way of giving their sex life a "tune-up."

I recommend this ritual to couples for two reasons. First, it frees up your attention during lovemaking so that you can include *both* your own *and* your partner's experience within your awareness at one time. Second, it teaches your body, in a very subtle way, how to contain a higher and finer state of excitation or responsiveness. In other words, you tend to become a more finely tuned instrument for exchanging energy with others.

— *Massage*

Most of us need a lot more touching and caressing than we ever get. Massaging your partner is a good way to express unselfish caring. It serves as a reminder of the joy of simply giving pleasure to another. Many people use sex as a way of trying to get nurturance, when a really loving massage would be more satisfying. When the need to receive nurturance is confused with the need for sex, neither need really gets satisfied. Sex involves mutual attunement, whereas the need for nurturance involves one person giving while the other receives.

If two people are trying to fulfill their needs for nurturance via sexual intercourse, a covert power struggle may occur about who will give and who will receive. In massage no such confusion occurs. As a result, both can enjoy their respective roles fully, without feeling any sense of competition.

There are many techniques or schools of massage and many useful self-help books on the subject. My advice to couples wishing to expand their mutual openness via massage is to read a good book on the subject *and* to use your own intuition about how to do it.

When first practicing the art of massage with a partner, ask for feedback frequently. And be sure to take turns giving and receiving, though not necessarily on the same day. Often it is best to space your massages so that on one occasion you give the massage and on the other occasion you receive. That way, no one has to hop up and give a massage right after receiving one. This teaches you that it is okay to simply receive. People who have difficulty being totally receptive can benefit most from this ritual.

— *One-Way Sex*

One-way sex is very similar to massage in that one person is the pleasure-giver while the other receives. The difference is that one-way sex has an explicitly erotic focus. Your aim is to turn your partner on. But unlike two-way "regular" sex, you can give your partner your undivided attention. This can be very freeing for both of you. It can also give you a fuller appreciation of how to pleasure your partner, knowledge that you can then use in regular sex.

People who have trouble reaching orgasm in regular sex often find that it is easy in one-way sex. They are not distracted by attempting to please their partners or by trying to synchronize their responses. They are free to go at their own pace as long as they are able to communicate their preferences to their partners.

With most couples, one person tends to reach orgasm more quickly or easily than the other. This can cause them to feel considerable tension regarding their sex life. One-way sex can serve a valuable therapeutic function in such situations. It helps the slower member of the pair to enjoy sex fully, no matter how long it takes. And it helps the faster one to appreciate and understand the other's sexual rhythms and pleasure zones.

In setting the stage for one-way sex, atmosphere is very important. If you are to be the giver on this particular occasion, you might want to take charge of providing a romantic atmosphere in advance of bringing your partner into the room. Let your partner feel that he or she is in capable, loving hands. Really get into the spirit of giving, and let your enjoyment of your partner's pleasure show. If you are uncertain about what would give your partner pleasure, ask. Or you might just do what you think would offer pleasure, and then ask for feedback about what you're doing. ''Multiple-choice'' questions work best here because they require little thought on the receiver's part, and because some people have difficulty articulating what they want in lovemaking. ''Would you like me to do this harder or softer?'' is an example.

One-way sex can sometimes turn into two-way sex in mid-stream. If this occurs, fine. But remember that one-way sex is not a second-best substitute for two-way sex. It is rather a nice thing to do together for a change of pace.

— *Balancing and Harmonizing Your Inner Polarities*
Sex can be a means of balancing the masculine, feminine, and various other polar energies within yourself. Making love is an act which harmonizes disparate energies — between yourself and your partner most obviously, but also within yourself in a more subtle way. Your partner in a sense symbolizes your other half. Thus, when you are attuned to your partner, you are also tuning up your own energy system.

In lovemaking, when you feel your body and your being uniting with your partner, imagine too that a similar unification is occurring within each of you. Imagine that your various parts are blending together into a harmonious whole.

As this unification ritual continues over time with the same partner, you may find the nature of your sex drive changing. It may become more relaxed, less urgent, and as a result, may seem less passionate. Don't become alarmed or think you are losing your sexual vitality. You are undergoing a transformation in the meaning of sex in your life. Sex is becoming less a way of overcoming separateness and aloneness, and more a way of celebrating the unification process occurring within you. You are now literally *making* love with your partner; that is, the two of you together are *creating* love that can then radiate outward from you both into the world around you.

All the rituals described here can be seen as ways of removing the armor from one's sexual persona, ways to become more energetically present to another. Usually when you open yourself more fully to your partner, your sexual pleasure increases. It may also occur, however, that you become more aware of certain sexual hungers and dependency needs you didn't know you had. This may feel uncomfortable at first. But if you can recognize these perhaps baby-like feelings as part of the normal opening-up process, then you won't feel the need to avoid these things or hide them from your partner. While it is true that some partners may be scared away when such a deep level of intimacy is reached, most people can accept in you anything you can accept in yourself.

# eleven: Bosses, Co-Workers, and Other Sex Objects

*TIME* recently informed us that "the sexual revolution is over." Perhaps, but in most *workplaces* it never even got started. The average office, shop or factory is not a very sexy place. The work ethic, which is the religion of capitalism, dictates that sexuality is to be left at home when setting out for a day's labor.

A kind of double standard exists in the expression of sexuality at work, however. A man is supposed to cover his sexuality underneath a three-piece suit or other uniform attire. A woman is often encouraged to display her sexual attractiveness, as long as it isn't done blatantly. Women are allowed to look sexy especially if they are employed in secretarial, reception, or similar roles which serve decorative as well as utilitarian functions. Such encouragement of female sexual attractiveness can be seen as a way of keeping a woman in her place. Men, who set the norms in most work settings, know how to deal with an attractive woman. They often have a harder time with a powerful woman.

When I was on the graduate school faculty of a large Eastern university, I encountered many male graduate students, about my age or a little older, who had difficulty with my position of authority over them. It was not unusual for

161

these men to attempt to shift a discussion from their doctoral dissertations to the possibility of a sexual liaison. The effort usually took one of several predictable forms: a declaration of being turned on to me as a woman; a suggestion that we expand our essentially mentor-mentee relationship to include a sexual aspect; a confession of inability to concentrate on the matter at hand.

While I was initially a bit nonplussed, I soon learned to respond with detachment and gentle firmness. Regardless of any genuine sexual attraction the man might have felt toward me, I am sure that the essential purpose of his gesture was not to get me into bed, but to get me into a position where he felt more my equal, rather than my student. By focusing on my femaleness in relation to his maleness, he could perhaps avoid dealing with my competence or my capacity to challenge his ideas.

During one of these encounters, when a male student about ten years older than I confessed fantasies of taking me to bed, I looked directly into his eyes and replied, "That's not what you want most. Mostly you want my respect." He smiled sheepishly and admitted that he was more confident with me as a sexual conquest than as a challenging woman whose professional respect and approval he desperately wanted.

Several decades ago anthropologist Margaret Mead made the observation that men are "unsexed" by failure and women are unsexed by success. Mead held that men feel less masculine when they regard themselves as failures, while women feel less feminine when they see themselves as successful.

My research and experience tell me that times are changing, especially for women. Today neither males nor females prefer the underling position, although women may be more graceful in accepting it when they have to. When a woman has organizational authority over a man, the man will often feel uncomfortable, but usually the woman will not. It is becoming rather unusual to find women in the workplace who lament their triumphs and successes over men.

We once expected successful females to feel like the little girl in John Greeleaf Whittier's poem:

> "I'm sorry that I spelt the word
> I hate to go above you
> Because," the brown eyes lower fell,
> "Because, you see, I love you."

That day seems to be passing. Yet there are still large discontinuities in the expectations most people hold for successful women. Women are supposed to retain their femininity and yet adapt their thinking and actions to a male-dominated world. Such contradictory expectations leave each individual woman in a somewhat ambiguous position, trying to achieve results using her competence rather than her sexuality, and yet wishing to be regarded as feminine.

Not long ago I heard about a female boss, supervisor of eleven male employees, who seemed caught in this whirlpool of changing expectations. Bernice was a legendary figure in her industry, in more ways than one. At 48, she was vibrant, sexy, and confident in her abilities. In her company, women in positions of high corporate responsibility were a rarity. And Bernice was a rarity among rarities. A woman with virtually no sexual inhibitions, she never worried about how her outrageous sexual exhibitions might affect others in her company. Co-workers tell of knocking on her half-open office door and finding her in the midst of a passionate embrace with one of her male employees. The men talked freely in the office about their minor sexual conquests with Bernice. She never went to bed with any of them, preferring to limit her sexual favors to "fooling around" in her office.

Most of the men in that office had never worked for a woman before, and they were uncomfortable doing so. None of their wives worked, and they liked it that way. They may have been comfortable with a woman telling them to pick up their clothes, but they didn't like being evaluated by a woman at performance appraisal time. So they made Bernice an object of sexual conquest. And she was only too happy to oblige, for it made her day at work much more agreeable to have many admiring men awaiting her feminine attentions.

Like many high-achieving women, Bernice was more confident of her technical expertise than of her sexual attractiveness. This made her perhaps more vulnerable to her employees' sexual overtures than she might otherwise have been.

Was Bernice "unsexed" by success? Apparently not! Yet on closer examination, it seems she may have been colluding with her male employees to keep the woman "in her place."

Were the men who worked for Bernice unsexed by having a female boss? Again, apparently not. Yet why did their office look like a Freudian playroom of adolescent sexuality? Were they perhaps compensating for something, trying to make themselves seem more powerful than they actually felt?

Some people feel more confident of their sexuality than of their competence. Others are sure of their competence, but uncertain of their sexual potency or attractiveness. Sometimes a work situation, such as not winning a promotion or having to perform meaningless work, can exacerbate existing self-doubts. Such a condition may stimulate the use of sexuality or power to re-establish feelings of self-esteem.

Bernice felt more sure of her power than of her sexual attractiveness. Her employees used this situation to gain a feeling of potency at work, a feeling that many of them were not able to get from the work itself.

Some people use sex in the workplace to help compensate for a lack of confidence in their abilities or a lack of meaningfulness in the work itself. People in positions of power, like Bernice, may use sex to compensate for self-doubts which are more personal than work-related.

In the past, it has been the province of men to take advantage of their positions of power to gain sexual favors. In the future, as Bernice has shown, gender will be no obstacle to opportunities for using power to get sex. But as Bernice's story also demonstrates, both parties may have something to gain, temporarily, from the blurring of sexual and authority boundaries.

Until recently, men have been accused of sexual harrassment, while women often were characterized as power seekers who created sexual liaisons to obtain influence or job favors. When we better understand the organizational dynamics which lead to such behavior, however, we may stop accusing one another and start dealing with the roots of the problem: most people fear others who are different, and those in power tend to want to keep it for themselves.

Many of these problems will be solved when the workplace has changed to the point of including fairly equal numbers of males and females in positions of authority. Then men will find dealing with powerful women a normal everyday occurrence and no longer will feel a need to put a woman ''in her place'' so they can deal with her in old familiar ways.

With more women in high-ranking positions, aspiring young women will have female mentors as available to them as males, making the use of sexuality to climb the career ladder unnecessary or obsolete. By then, women will see many successful role models of their own gender in highly respected positions, alleviating the need for a woman to prove herself just because she is a woman.

As men and women become accustomed to working side by side as equals, neither will feel the need to exploit the other to validate their competence or attractiveness. Work relationships will more often be based on respect than on manipulation or domination. When this occurs, both will be freer to enjoy their maleness and femaleness, within bounds of course, as a way of adding zest to the work relationship. This can occur once sex becomes less useful as a tool for gaining power or for keeping another from becoming too powerful. A woman will then be able to more freely express

her femininity without fear that it will detract from her power.
A man will be freer to express his masculinity because he is
no longer tempted to use it to gain sexual favors, or because
he no longer fears being accused of sexual harrassment.

These are times of transition with respect to the
appropriate expression of sexuality in the workplace. A few
generations ago, men and women were rarely found working
side by side. Now, most work environments present us with
the opportunity to appreciate or ignore each other's sexuality,
and to express or inhibit the expression of our own. There are
no universally agreed upon rules for sexual conduct in the
workplace. Organizations and professional associations try to
monitor their members' sexual conduct, but there is a great
gap between organizational dictum and individual action.

## Business Affairs

In a time of such changes in sexual mores, it is inevitable
that sexual expression between co-workers can move beyond
the bounds of propriety and efficiency. This often occurs when
a man and a woman find themselves cooperating intensely on
a project over some period of time. As they get to know each
other better and better, feelings of closeness can easily
develop. They may realize that they see more of each other
than they do of their respective spouses, since work is such a
big part of their lives.

Most companies discourage or forbid sexual
relationships between co-workers. This can lead the lovers
into a dishonest relationship with their supervisors. And, of
course, if one or both are married, even more people will be
affected and perhaps deceived.

If you do become sexually involved over a period of time
with someone at work, in most cases honesty with your
supervisor is a good idea, particularly if you work in a small
shop or organization with little privacy or anonymity. I
advocate this for two reasons: because it is going to come to
light sooner or later if the relationship is indeed serious; and

because most bosses will sense that you are trying to hide something from them, and they may jump to the wrong conclusions about what you are hiding. These conclusions or false impressions could hurt you more than the truth. Of course, such revelations are not without risk, but you took the biggest risk when you became involved with a co-worker in the first place!

As you plan to approach a supervisor with this news, there are some ways that work better than others. I assume you want to end up with the boss on your side. This is most likely to occur if you sincerely seek the boss's counsel on the matter. It is in his or her interest to help you do the best work you can do; so the focus should be on how your love affair affects your *job performance* or that of others near you. This is the heart of the matter. If the conversation begins to get off track, bring it back to whether your supervisor perceives any change in your job performance. Be open to your supervisor's viewpoint. That's the best way to insure that he or she will be open to yours. But be clear within yourself before you go to talk to your boss as to which is more important, your job or your affair.

## What's A Boss To Do?

If you as a supervisor suspect two of your employees to be sexually involved, I suggest waiting a while before intervening. Observe as objectively as you can whether or not this situation hampers either one's job performance. Often productivity is enhanced by working with someone you love; so be open to this possibility. If you discern that their work is suffering, approach the encounter tentatively and supportively. Begin from the attitude that you all have a job to do together, and you need the best from each other. Assume that they too wish to do a good job. Whether this is true or not, expressing it as an expectation can't hurt anything. Stay focused on how their liaison affects their work or their relationships with other co-workers, including yourself.

Before embarking on such a potentially difficult interview, spend some time getting clear within yourself about your various reactions to the situation. Do you detect any envy or feelings of being excluded? Do you feel disapproval or silent support? Is their behavior something you can empathize with, or is it totally beyond your understanding? Reflecting on such questions as these will help you to be more aware and focused during the interview.

It is easy advise, ''Don't get your honey where you get your money,'' as a Black American colloquialism suggests. But life in the world of work just isn't that simple. It happens. So you need to be prepared to deal with it if it does occur. If you resent employees who bring you face to face with such a situation, your effectiveness in dealing with the matter will suffer. Try to make your values known to your employees as a matter of policy before any such case comes up. Let the consequences for violation of your policies be known as well. And then, be prepared for anything!

## You Are Not Alone

When one or both of the lovers are married, it is important to realize that a business affair may signal the beginning of the end for that marriage. Whether you are single or married, if you are involved with a married co-worker, remember that your behavior affects more than just the two of you. What you do creates ripples in the lives of others, even if you think you have a very well-kept secret.

Whatever the benefits of your on-the-job relationship, there are bound to be costs, to the two of you, and to those closest to you — at work and at home. Don't assume you will get away with it without paying a price. Nobody does.The struggle you experience may be fuel for growth, but struggle you will.

## The Home-Office Connection

People whose lives are rigidly compartmentalized into home vs. work, or co-workers vs. friends, often find their hearts similarly compartmentalized. Often, for example, one sees work friends only during the workday and family only evenings and weekends. An alternative approach is to let your spouse know about your work and let your co-workers, especially opposite sex co-workers, meet your spouse. Then you are less likely to find yourself in a situation where your work relationships are in competition with your family, or vice versa.

If you are going on a business trip with a co-worker of the opposite sex, for example, why not arrange for the co-worker and your spouse to meet and get to know one another? Then they are more apt to feel like allies rather than competitors for your attention. Such contact may also reduce your own temptation to ''stray'' while on the road. By encouraging your co-worker to become friendly with your spouse, you do much to prevent unnecessary family tensions. This assumes, of course, that you are not contemplating a ''business affair'' with this co-worker, in which case the tensions are in order.

A friend of mine, Charlie Ames, who traveled frequently with his female research assistant, made a regular practice of inviting his wife to lunch with him and his assistant before any scheduled out-of-town trip. While he and his assistant did not have a love affair, they did have a very close friendship based on their work together. Charlie's wife Shelley knew this, and had felt rather unhappy about Charlie's relationship with this attractive single woman until Charlie began to take preventive action. Through these occasional lunches, Shelley and Charlie's assistant developed a friendship of their own, and sometimes they even had lunch together without Charlie. Once Shelley no longer felt excluded from the relationship between her husband and his co-worker, she no longer felt threatened by it.

Most close business relationships between members of the opposite sex do not involve physical sexual relationships. Nevertheless, they can pose a real threat to a marriage if not handled wisely. Charlie's actions were extremely important in promoting a trusting relationship between his wife and his assistant, and alleviating unnecessary tension in his marriage.

The subject I've called ''business affairs'' is obviously too complex to make rules about. The important things are (1) that you use your situation to grow in your love and understanding of yourself and others, and (2) that you take care not to hurt others in the process. Expression of our sexuality is in many ways a child-like pleasure. Nevertheless, it requires the fullest measure of adult responsibility in evaluating and accepting the consequences of your actions.

## Does Sexuality Have a Place on the Job?

Given the shifting expectations regarding sex roles and sexuality, what sorts of behaviors are appropriate for men and women who work together?

The following list of *do's* and *don'ts* brings the philosophy of earlier chapters to bear on this question:

*Do* allow yourself to feel your maleness or femaleness while at work. Your sexual energy is really synonymous with your vitality, your *joie de vivre*. When you feel like a sexual being, you feel more whole and alive, and are more fun to be around. Do whatever you need to do to help yourself feel attractive, especially to yourself. This may mean wearing clothes that fit well, or colors that appeal to you. It may mean getting enough sleep or exercise. Your body will tell you what it needs in order to feel vibrant.

*Don't* draw undue attention to your physical self. You can be attractive without attracting attention. If you feel the need to attract attention to yourself by means of your physical attributes, perhaps you need to ask yourself if you are compensating for some other lack in relationship to your work (unless you happen to be a body builder or a model!). People will generally trust and respect you more when your physical presence exudes a quality of confidence rather than flashiness.

*Do* offer nurturance, warmth, humor and praise to the people with whom you work. Give them many of the same courtesies you would give to a lover, in other words. You don't

always have to be businesslike just because you are in
business together.

*Don't* confuse caring, admiration, or even sexual attraction
with sexual intimacy. Even if your opposite sex co-worker
seems to appreciate you more than your spouse does, for
example, that does not mean you should become lovers or
mates. There's more to a good sexual relationship than
attraction; the setting in which your relationship occurs and
the other people affected by it are among the important
considerations.

*Do* express your attractiveness with grace and openness.
Allow yourself to receive and acknowledge the appreciation of
others.

*Don't* ignore the effect you have on others. For example, if
someone becomes infatuated with you due to your warmth
and openness, it is partly your responsibility. It is not enough
to say, ''I can't help it if my behavior turns other people on.''
You *can* help it. It's up to you to do what you can to discourage
inappropriate infatuations.

*Do* try to nurture the development of junior workers or
those who are new to the job. Be willing to offer your
mentorship when the situation calls for it. Take care also to
avoid giving special favors only to opposite sex co-workers.

*Don't* expect other special favors in return for such
assistance. If you give someone your help or your knowledge,
give it freely.

*Do* let your opposite sex co-workers know your feelings
about traditionally chivalrous behaviors — such as opening
doors for a woman, holding out her chair at the table or paying
for her meal. Many men are confused these days about what
women want and expect. Likewise, many women are confused
about what to expect from men. Rather than applying a rigid
set of rules, begin by observing what you really want to do or
have done for you, regardless of what you think the other
expects. For example, if you really want to pay for your
co-worker's meal, fine; offer to do so. But if you are just trying
to do ''the right thing,'' forget it. There is no *right thing* in
these times of change.

The challenge for men and women today is to find out about each other as individuals with unique talents and preferences, without relying on gender stereotypes. This requires a level of honesty and clarity that can occur only when both sexes feel that they are beyond the power struggle.

# twelve: Toward Resolution of the Power Struggle

**Have you ever** found yourself in the middle of an argument between two people you cared about — where you could see value in both viewpoints? Frustrating, isn't it? To you both ways are partially valid. You can see them as part of a larger picture. But each of the adversaries is focused on a particular detail rather than the whole picture.

George and Linda Catton are in disagreement about how to motivate their 16-year old son Tony to stay in high school rather than quitting. Linda says, "Let's talk to Tony and see why he wants to quit and then take it from there." George objects, "Absolutely not! This would only reinforce Tony's idea about quitting. We need to state our position clearly and strongly. We simply will not permit him to quit." "But," protests Linda, "we want him to know we care about him and his feelings, that we're not just being arbitrary." "Oh, come on!" shouts George, "Tony knows we love him. He needs firmness right now, not coddling."

As the objective witness to this argument, you can probably see some validity in each of their positions. *Both* caring *and* firmness seem to be called for in this situation. How, then, did these two parents, who love each other and

173

their son, get so polarized in their positions? Why is it so hard
for them to see with the wider perspective that we have? They
act as if they fear losing something if they were to recognize
the validity in each other's views. What might they lose? And
why is this matter so important to each of them?

## The Either-Or World of Linda and George

According to the way George and Linda see the world,
you are *either* tough with your son, *or* you are tender. And in
their family, it is Linda who provides the tenderness and
George the toughness. Neither is very comfortable with the
other's way.

Linda, a petite, cherubic woman, has never learned how
to be tough or even firm when necessary. She grew up in a
wealthy suburb of a large mid-western city, the kind of
environment where young people were chauffeured and
pampered and given every advantage without having to work
very hard. Soon after leaving the nest of her parents' home,
midway through her sophomore year of college, she met and
married George. She never had the experience of fending for
herself in an unsupportive environment. All her life she has
been surrounded by love and support.

She was first attracted to square-built, burly George
partly because his approach to life seemed so unusual, so
foreign and therefore fascinating. He had grown up in a
multi-racial Brooklyn neighborhood of high-rise apartments
and small shops. His extra-curricular education had been on
the streets and in pool halls; hers had been at the family's
lakeside cottage or at after-school classes in piano, dance and
elocution. She was fascinated by his rugged, self-sufficient,
almost tough manner. She felt protected by George's
confident firmness in dealing with the world, though at the
same time, it did make her a little uncomfortable.

George had been attracted to Linda's softness and sense
of ease about life. He would never have consciously wished to
be this way himself, but in a woman, he liked a soft and
tender manner. When Linda cared for him in her gentle way,

George felt safe and secure in a way he had never known in his entire life, not even as an infant.

As he lived with Linda over time, however, George became more and more critical of her sweet and gentle style. Linda could never punish or even strongly reprimand Tony. When George returned home from work every evening, she would report to him Tony's infractions and misbehaviors of the day, leaving him with the task of disciplining the boy. Linda's gentleness could be downright mushy at times! George also began to notice that she habitually depended upon him to deal with the more difficult situations in their life, like the time she coaxed him into going to the PTA meeting on her behalf to protest against the new busing regulation, or the time she asked him to rescue her after a vacuum cleaner salesman had fast-talked her into purchasing $1000 more merchandise than she really needed.

George feared that if Tony, a slightly-built, sensitive youth, came too much under his mother's influence, he would grow up with no mind of his own, depending on others to fight his battles.

George and Linda's differences in style and opinion are reflected in a typical breakfast conversation:

George: I think I'll wear my old khaki blazer and some navy blue slacks to the Nash's for that garden party tomorrow.

Linda: That sounds fine. Whatever you feel comfortable in, dear. I'm not sure what I should wear. What do you think I should wear?

G: You look really sexy and feminine in that yellow sundress with the bare back. I'd like you to wear that.

L: Okay, I'll wear that.... How's the coffee?

G: Tepid. You know I like my coffee very strong and very hot. What happened?

L: I guess I'm distracted this morning, honey, Here, I'll make you another cup — real hot and strong, just like you (nestling close to him, cradling his head in her arms).

G: Hey! You're going to get lipstick on my collar.

L: Why can't you just relax, George?

G: I don't want you to get distracted again and burn my

coffee. And besides I've got a tough day ahead of me. Got to fire that new foreman. So I can't go in there all sweet and cuddly.

L: Can't you shift gears when you get to work? It would be nice if you didn't have to use me to work yourself up to fire someone.

G: You've never done anything like that in your life. You wouldn't understand...it reminds me of how different we are when it comes to our son.

L: (narrowing her eyes as she looks at him) What do you mean, George?

G: I mean that you think everything comes easy. That it's all okay either way, whether he stays in school or quits.

L: No, I don't, George. I think you're right in wanting him to stay in school. I sort of do, too. But I don't know. These days school may not be relevant to boys like Tony. At least that's what I read in the magazines.

G: You read that? Where? What magazine? You get an idea from a book or a magazine and you agree with it. You get another idea from me, and you agree with that. Where are your own ideas?

L: I'm only asking that we hear Tony's side of the picture.

G: Then you'd just have another opinion to agree with. What are you made of, woman? Jelly?

L: Someone has to keep you from totally dominating your son. He's not you, George. He has his own ways, thank God.

G: Just be careful. In protecting him from me, you may be raising a boy who's gonna need protection all his life.

L: Here's your coffee...strong enough?

G: Much better. Thanks.

As we get a closer look at George and Linda's relationship, we begin to suspect that their struggle over Tony staying in school is simply one battleground for coming to terms with their differences:

— Linda never developed the capacity for expressing strong feelings or opinions. As a child, she learned to gain self-esteem by being nice and by getting other people to like her.

— George never developed the capacity to feel empathy or tenderness for others. As a child, he learned to gain self-esteem by being powerful, by getting people to do things his way.

— Linda wishes George would show more tenderness with her. She's getting tired of doing all the giving.

— George wishes Linda would learn to stand up for a position instead of being so wishy-washy. He gets tired of always being the bad guy.

— Linda doesn't want her son Tony to model himself after the one-sided "Marlboro Man" image as her husband has done. Nor does she want Tony to feel dominated by his father.

— George doesn't want Tony to grow up into a mealy-mouthed weakling. He hopes Tony will always have the courage to speak his own mind. He fears what may happen if Linda continues to overprotect Tony.

— Linda was originally attracted to George's firmness, but now she is feeling that he can be absolutely rigid and unyielding at times.

— George was originally attracted to Linda's tenderness, but he is now beginning to feel that she has no mind of her own, that she is too dependent upon him to define how she should think and act.

## Giving Up and Gaining Power

George and Linda's power struggle, while focused on their son, involves a great deal more than Tony staying in school. Each is fighting to have the partner recognize and validate his or her point of view and way of being. Without this respect or recognition, George and Linda feel powerless with each other, unable to influence each other's feelings and actions. Thus, even more basic and important than the struggle for power is the wish for acceptance. Everyone alive wishes to be loved or accepted for themselves, just as they are. This is the most simple if not the most common of all human concerns: "I just want to be accepted as I am."

Embedded in this simple wish is another, less obvious, but just as common concern: ''I want to be free to express myself fully, all my various aspects, traits, feelings and foibles.'' This is what is meant by the drive toward wholeness. Biologists have called it, ''the drive in living matter to perfect itself.'' Everyone seeks a place or a relationship or a state of mind where they feel accepted and relaxed enough to be themselves, and where, as they discover or develop new qualities in themselves, they feel free to express these as well. The drive toward wholeness motivates us to seek a sense of harmony within ourselves and between ourselves and others. It is a drive which is unfulfilled in nearly every human being alive. It accounts for a great deal of what goes on in so-called sexual attraction. And it is behind much of a person's motivation to work, to be productive or creative.

Self-acceptance and acceptance by others tend to go hand in hand. Either one can pave the way for the other. When we feel accepted by others, we tend to feel more accepting of ourselves. And when we are able to accept ourselves, others tend to accept us as well.

George's battle with Linda around his toughness may very well have parallels in his relationships with his co-workers. When you are moving toward the expression of qualities you have never before felt free enough to express, acceptance of these qualities by others often becomes an issue for you wherever you go, in love, at work, with your children, with your friends.

George was able, after a time, to recognize the inner struggle that was underlying his struggle with Linda. George slowly began to see that he, like Linda, had a need to be supported and cared for by others, even a need to be liked the way people liked her. This led him to the awareness of a tender side in his own personality. He realized that he had been protesting against this quality in Linda and in Tony partly because of his discomfort with these sorts of feelings in himself. He began to allow Linda to be his teacher rather than his adversary.

This change, of course, had a big impact on George's relationship with Linda. It also significantly altered the tone of his conversations with Linda about Tony's schooling. George was now able to admit the value of Linda's suggestion that they discuss their feelings with Tony, without abandoning his equally strong commitment that Tony should stay in school. George is affirming a growing comfort with his own impulse toward tenderness. As he comes to accept tenderness in himself, he also gains a new, more confident and powerful feeling about himself. It is as if some new energy is liberated when one comes to see and accept some formerly hidden aspect. This change within George also places him in a new relationship to others whom he might once have judged as soft or wishy-washy. He has more compassion for others as he comes to accept himself more fully.

As George becomes more accepting of Linda's style, she stops fighting to be accepted by him, allowing herself to be more open to his viewpoint. In so doing, she is not only changing her attitude toward her husband, but is also taking a step toward becoming more comfortable with her own impulse toward firmness.

As George and Linda come to accept more of themselves and each other, their life together becomes infinitely more peaceful. They are also able to see and accept both the firm and soft sides of their son, thus helping him to develop an easier balance between these two qualities.

## "...You Can See Forever..."

You can get out of a power struggle in just two steps: open your vision wide enough to see the other's viewpoint, and allow this opening to soften your attachment to your original point of view.

When George is able to open his mind to Linda, Linda becomes more open to him. Both stop focusing on a narrow detail and allow a more complete picture to emerge. Now each can see more than they allowed themselves to see before. Because they are now more open to one another's influence, they each gain a feeling of potency in the relationship.

Opening your vision is a process of relaxing, letting go of whatever detail you may have been be fixed upon, and taking in more of the total panorama. If you see your differences with another person from a broader perspective, you can appreciate them as complementary, rather than antagonistic. When you are open to your differences in style or opinion, rather than fearful or resistant, you gain power to deal intelligently with them. When you respond to differences with anger, denial, self-righteousness or the like, you have no adequate means for resolving them.

You gain a new kind of power when you give up having to have your own way. You become more able to see things as they are, and there is new room in your world for varying perspectives and a wider range of information.

"But," you protest, "if I let go too easily, people will walk all over me! Someone has to look out for my interests." Perhaps this is true. But the attitude you hold as you assert your interests or point of view is of crucial importance. Do you assert yourself with an attitude that assumes, "She's not really interested in what I have to say. She just wants to get her own way with me." Or as you assert yourself, are you feeling, "I know he wants to understand me, so it is important for me to be as clear and honest as possible."

Do you feel fearful and defensive or open and worthy of respect? Remember that *how* you express yourself is as important as what you say. You will probably find that when you let go of the fearful, demanding I-have-to-have-it-my-way attitude, people more easily and naturally give to you without you doing anything special to get it. When your *way of being* communicates an attitude of respect and openness, you draw to you respect and openness from others.

When George was able to surrender and allow himself to embrace Linda's viewpoint alongside his own, Linda stopped fighting him. She began to pay more attention to him instead of holding so tightly and defensively to just her own opinion. This enabled George to have a stronger impact on her than if he had continued to forcefully assert his view. When he had focused solely on his own opinion, Linda didn't hear him. When he admitted that his opinion was not the only one, Linda was able to stop defending herself and to relax enough to let George's views really make an impression on her.

Have you ever noticed that when you stop worrying about getting or finding something or someone, then it seems to magically appear? This is an illustration of a general principle of human relationships: what we attract to ourselves is a mirror of what we already are, that is, of our feelings and images of what we are. If you love and respect yourself, you attract love and respect. If we fear people are going to rip us off, people will seem to rip us off. If I hold to the idea, "people always ignore me," I will often find myself being ignored.

I have also found that the more emotional energy I feel about wishing others to change or behave a certain way, the more they tend to resist me. As a supervisor observing my employees work, the more I am critical of how they are doing the job, the more likely they are to botch the job (for me). The more urgently I ask my lover to join me in the garden to "*appreciate* the *beautiful* sunset," the less of the sunset's beauty he will experience, because my attachment to how he *should* feel interferes with his spontaneity. The urgency of my feelings, however subtly expressed, dominates the psychic space between us. He senses my lack of acceptance for him and for the moment as it is, and his openness to me and to the situation suffers accordingly.

My partner's resistance to me in such moments is not born entirely of stubbornness, however. He is actually showing me that my need for things to be a certain way, in order to feel satisfied, is interfering with my ability to see and respond intelligently to how things are.

Have you ever noticed how happy people are usually happy no matter what their external circumstances? While unhappy people seem always to be looking for things to be different than they are? When you have to have things a certain way in order to be satisfied, you're bound to be dissatisfied most of the time. The most frustrated and angry

people in the world are people who are attached to having
their own way, while the happiest, most self-assured people,
in love or work, are those who have learned to take life as it
comes.

As we saw in the story of George and Linda, letting go of
attachment to your own way does not imply giving away your
power. It is more a case of choosing a different attitude about
the situation, consciously and powerfully: choosing to let go of
insistence on "getting what you want," realizing that "what
you've got" right now has much to offer you.

Only when you understand how to accept and use what
life offers you will you be granted new and different offerings.
As long as you refuse to accept life as it is, you will be
frustrated, wanting some future or seemingly unavailable
state of affairs. Letting go of attachment to your own way
really means accepting the way things are instead of hanging
on to how you wish they were. "How things are" often
includes recognition of uncomfortable feelings and qualities
within yourself that you have avoided. It also often includes
the fact of a real live other person in your life with wants and
rhythms that differ from your own. But once you learn to relax
with this fact, the differences may no longer make so much
difference.

The broader vision required to successfully resolve power
struggles may be gained in at least three specific ways: taking
back projections; looking for the softer feelings; and finding
something to agree about. I will discuss each of these in turn.

## Take It Back!

Whenever we find ourselves emotionally involved in
conflicts with others, it is probably an indication of unresolved
conflicts within ourselves. To become aware of such a hidden
aspect of personality, it is often necessary first to notice it in
another person. Sometimes we go even farther, consciously or
unconsciously, and *project* onto others those traits we prefer
not to acknowledge in ourselves.

If I tend to be angry and suspicious toward men, but would find that feeling unacceptable in myself, I might be extra-sensitive to noticing such behavior in other women. I may get irritated about the way another woman talks about men. Such a response may be a signal that there is some attitude within me that I have not acknowledged, but instead have projected onto other women.

George, in the example above, was unable to recognize his own latent inclinations toward tenderness and was therefore uncomfortable with what he considered to be Linda's wishy-washy style. Linda, because she could not express her capacity for firmness, found George to be rigid and unyielding. When George was able to take back the projection of his tenderness onto Linda, he became much more respecting of her ideas about how to deal with their son. As an added benefit, he also found that he was no longer dependent on her to provide all the tenderness in their relationship.

The projection mechanism shields a person from seeing or expressing feelings or traits that do not fit with the self image. It defends against new, uncomfortable or unacceptable aspects, which may be quite useful and attractive, but are out of awareness. Projection often shows itself through hypersensitivity and emotional displays. Such reactions, either favorable or unfavorable, will be directed toward a quality in others which the person seems unable to express.

Another example of how projection works can be seen in the story of Calvin and Hilda, a couple who have known each other only two years. Calvin is a man who likes to see himself as always calm and cool. He prides himself on his ability to remain unflustered in even the most challenging situations. There is one thing that really makes him uncomfortable, however, and that is Hilda's inability to relax. He is bothered by the amount of time she spends talking on the telephone. He feels she is entirely too compulsive about doing housework. He gets upset with how fast she eats her food. He is highly critical of the rapid-fire manner of her speech and her frequent gesticulation as she talks.

Given all his irritability with Hilda, could it be that Calvin himself has not really learned to relax? Perhaps because he becomes anxious so easily, he is hypersensitive to Hilda's state of relaxation or tension.

Couples often get into power struggles of this sort. Calvin cannot admit his own anxiety, so he projects a feeling of agitation onto Hilda and tries to get her to calm down. Hilda, for her part, is bothered by Calvin's inertia. Because she harbors a secret fear of her own passivity, she has become extra-sensitive to this quality in others. She has come to regard herself as very active and vivacious, and tends to project onto Calvin "lifelessness and inactivity" as a way of avoiding contact with these feelings in herself. In their struggle, she usually tries to get Calvin to be more energetic, to get out more and do things. As he tries to get her to slow down, she attempts to get him to speed up.

Initially, Hilda was probably attracted to Calvin's calmness and he to her vivacity. But with time and an ever-growing resistance to their differences, the attraction turned to repulsion. Knowing another and allowing ourselves to be known over time can bring an increased tendency for formerly unknown parts of oneself to exert pressure to be known and acknowledged. This pressure often feels as if something threatening were about to occur; a psychological counter-effort may be launched to try to prevent the emergence of unfamiliar qualities or feelings.

In intimate relationships especially, it often occurs that after the more superficial layers of our personalities have been seen and accepted, the deeper, generally hidden, layers begin to press for attention. As our more superficial projections are taken back, thus becoming conscious, new still-hidden dimensions press for attention. Deeper and more unfamiliar projections demand to be admitted into awareness.

This is why the really difficult power struggles don't occur right away in relationships. The more we know and trust one another, the more likely it is that formerly hidden aspects of our personalities will emerge. This is actually a natural healthy part of the growth process of any relationship.

In order for Calvin and Hilda to move beyond the power struggle of blame and counter-blame, one or both must break their habitual cycle with some new thoughts: "Maybe the thing I'm bothered by in her is a signal that I have a blind spot about myself." "Maybe it's not him who is responsible for my irritation...maybe I am responsible."

The next step in breaking the cycle is to communicate this change of attitude to your partner. Let her know that you are now engaged in looking at the "log in your own eye instead of the speck in your brother's."

You may now wish to simply observe your negative emotional reactions for a period of time. Notice what it is about his behavior that pushes your irritation button. Notice your exact thoughts and feelings. What do you say to yourself about her motives? What do you feel, and where in your body does this feeling occur? Does this situation remind you of anything that has ever happened before in your life?

Simple but careful self-observation is the most effective route to self-knowledge. But remember to carry on your observations in a spirit of seeking to understand yourself rather than to change yourself. If you are a careful and sincere self-scientist, your observations will lead you where you need to go.

Calvin will notice *his own* anxiety when Hilda starts to talk or eat too fast. He may notice also that he then tends to automatically shut down his feelings and withdraw into a private world of his own. He may then observe himself judging and theorizing about what Hilda needs to learn in order to become calmer and happier. Then he may see himself begin preaching to her. After repeated observations of this pattern of events, Calvin will find himself waking up to parts of himself that had been unconscious or asleep, such as his characteristic way of managing his anxiety — by blaming Hilda. When this awareness occurs, he will find he has access to a greater range of feelings in himself and consequently, compassion for more different types of people.

Projection causes us to deny certain aspects of ourselves, positive or negative, and attribute these to others. Some people have difficulty owning up to positive or powerful aspects of themselves, as in the well-publicized "fear of success" pattern. As we saw earlier, Linda Catton was attracted to George's firmness, never recognizing that she had this same quality hidden within herself. After a time such dependence on her husband led her to resent him for the very quality that she had once so appreciated. When she was able to reclaim her own firmness — to take back the projection onto George — she gained new power, and overcame one more power struggle.

Most couples are attracted because the partners admire certain qualities in each other. For many, like George and Linda and Calvin and Hilda, the partners come together because they secretly wish to *have* one or more of the admired traits. They have disowned or denied expression of this quality in themselves, and seek, often not even consciously, to regain it through partnership.

As they help each other to develop these qualities, the power struggle resolves itself. The more they recognize and accept all aspects of their own personalities, the more understanding and accepting they become of each other, and of all others. An other doesn't seem quite so "other" when one can recognize oneself over there.

## Looking for the Softer Feelings

Power struggles are often characterized by hurt or angry behavior accompanied by an attitude of blame: "You hurt me!" "What you did ruined my day!" These hard, sharp accusations are usually rooted in soft, difficult-to-articulate feelings, such as a longing to be closer or a fear of losing the other's love or respect. When partners are able to recognize the feelings underneath the surface conflict, the power struggle often dissolves into mutual understanding.

## Bob and Rhonda's Struggle Beneath the Struggle

Bob and Rhonda, a couple in their early 40's, had been married for eight years when they first came to see me for counseling. Although they had weathered many conflicts in their years together, their present struggle felt more threatening to the relationship than had any of the others. They came to me in the heat of a battle over whether or not to open their marriage to other sex partners. She wanted to, and he didn't. And they were both absolutely adamant in their positions.

Each had developed an impressive arsenal of accusations, attacks and insults designed to beat the other into submission. During our first session together, Bob led off by accusing Rhonda of being "genitally preoccupied.... Whenever things don't go well for us, she knows just what to do to make herself feel better and to get back at me!" Rhonda countered by telling Bob he was "just like my father, except my father knew how to make money!"

I was looking at two very hurt and angry people. Bob and Rhonda were trying to hurt each other as each felt he or she had been hurt. It was obvious they would never get through the power struggle this way. They needed to discover the softer, more vulnerable and sensitive feelings underlying Rhonda's wish for sexual variety and Bob's wish for more closeness. Each had to accept the possibility that there was more to their feelings than what they were able to express at the moment. I felt certain they were protecting some more vulnerable parts of themselves through their power struggle.

Rhonda and Bob saw this as an interesting and real possibility. Slowly and uncertainly at first, they began to look at feelings beyond the anger and hostility they had been throwing at each other, exploring what they loved about each other and their relationship.

Rhonda began to disclose that there was a part of herself that felt so completely fulfilled in her sexual relationship with Bob that she was afraid. She was afraid that if sometime he might leave her or be temporarily unavailable to her, she would feel helpless and adandoned. She confessed that whenever she was close to Bob for long uninterrupted periods of time, she felt this fear.

Listening to Rhonda's disclosure, Bob's visage became softer and more relaxed. As Bob came to understand the roots of Rhonda's desire for an open marriage, his accusations ceased and he began to show a sincere interest and concern for her feelings.

As Bob relaxed his pressure on her, Rhonda felt freer to confront herself and to really examine whether any of the things Bob had said about her might be true. When she no longer needed to fend off Bob's confrontations, she had more attention available for self-confrontation. As Rhonda looked more deeply at her motives for seeking an open marriage, she saw that it was her softer, "little girl side" that she had been protecting. And as she acknowledged and accepted her own fears and feelings of helplessness, she felt strangely less fearful and less helpless. Her attitude of greater self-acceptance acted as a kind of support for the little girl or vulnerable part of herself. This allowed her softer side to feel more cared for and therefore more able to express itself directly with tender, even hungry, feelings, rather than defensively in an attitude of self-protection.

When it was Bob's turn to look beneath his offensive-defensive protection system, he, too, discovered a softer aspect of his personality. As he searched beneath his hurt pride and angry accusations, he found in himself a feeling amazingly similar to Rhonda's, a growing feeling of dependency accompanied by a fear of being left. He shared with Rhonda the knee-jerk reaction he had whenever she would talk of being with other men, feeling too threatened to express himself softly or even rationally. He didn't want to lose her to another man, and wanted to be able to tell her that,

instead of verbally attacking her sexuality. Once he
recognized how this reaction was affecting Rhonda, he could
let go of his pride and accept his own softer feelings. Then he
was able to simply say what he wanted and didn't want,
instead of attacking and blaming.

It usually only takes one member of a partnership to
begin the change from blaming to softening. As long as the
two people have a basic caring for each other, one person's
opening and softening is enough to set the forces of change in
motion. When Rhonda admitted her tenderest feelings to
Bob, it was no longer necessary for him to try to batter away
at her defenses; her defenses had melted. This freed Bob to
pay attention to his own feelings, leading him to awareness of
formerly hidden feelings within himself.

## "There Must Be Something We Agree About!"

Usually power struggles are about means, not ends. They
center on *how* to make sure Johnny is healthy, not *whether* we
want a healthy child. Thus, Greg may advocate bribing
Johnny to eat his vegetables, while Sally may feel it is best to
leave the child alone. It is the *way*, not the destination that
causes friction between Greg and Sally.

If you and your partner or co-worker have different *styles*
of doing things, it is easy to confuse this with a difference in
*values*. A person with an extroverted, sociable style may see
the key to a happy marriage as having lots of friends around
all the time. A quieter, introverted person may feel that the
best way to nurture a relationship is with lots of intimate time
together as a couple alone. The goals are the same, but the
means are quite different.

If you and your partner can discover that your essential
aim in a conflict situation is the same, then you can begin to
work together, rather than against each other. Once a
common aim has been agreed upon, the next step is to adopt
the attitude that both positions contain something of value.
This more inclusive attitude validates both persons as
sincerely wanting the common aim to be achieved.

From such an attitude of positive expectations and good will, positive outcomes are more likely to follow. Each person feels recognized and valued, so energy is not wasted in fighting to be heard, that is, in fighting for power. You can move forward together with your attention on the problem at hand, bringing the resources of both to bear on the situation.

Sometimes, in order to arrive at an attitude of respect for the other's perspective, you need to find a way of putting yourself in your partner's position. See if you can take on the thoughts, feelings and life story of this other person. If you were him or her, why would you be holding this particular view? If you have trouble seeing your partner's viewpoint, ask for help. Find out, for example, what past experience led him or her to prefer to do things this way. Seek only to understand and empathize, not to evaluate or judge.

Once both of you have seen the situation from the viewpoint of the other, you have automatically enlarged each of your perspectives. Dialogue in search of a common course should now be more harmonious. If it isn't, go back again to seeking to better know your partner's position. This very act of sincerely empathizing with another leads that person to open up to you and your influence. This only works, of course, if your intentions are to really understand your partner, not to manipulate in order to get your way.

Sometimes things don't work out as smoothly as this, of course. Sometimes the stakes appear to be so high that partners' fears and irrationalities take over the situation. When a power struggle is extremely intense you find yourselves repeatedly hurting one another, gaining nothing. Sometimes the only thing left to do is for one person to *step outside* the struggle: "Let's stop doing this. I don't want us to keep on hurting each other like this, do you?" If both of you can feel your pain and helplessness about the situation at the same moment, you may have found the first point of agreement between you in a long time. And you may find that it *feels good* to agree for a change.

Your shared feeling of helplessness can lead to a shared feeling of relief. Since harmony and agreement almost always feel better than conflict, you may be moved to take a fresh look at whatever you were fighting about — to see if it really is reason for jeopardizing the relationship. If it is, you can go back to your positions, but if you find that the interruption affords a welcome and longed-for feeling of agreement, perhaps you will realize that the relationship is more important than the conflict of the moment. Agreement should not be sought at any cost — for example, your personal integrity — but it is important to know how to break an impasse and reach agreement if you wish to.

## You Get What You Give

Have you ever been in an argument and found that the more you bolstered up your position, the more the other person did the same? And the more you sincerely attempted to understand the other's position, the more he or she seemed willing to hear yours?

As we have already seen, you tend to get what you give. But why is this so? Why should attachment to one's own viewpoint cause conflict? Why can't I just stick to my view and the other stick to hers, and just let the best side win? After all, isn't that the way it's done in boxing and football?

Sticking to one's position does indeed tend to engender football- or boxinglike strategies on both sides. We try to strengthen ourselves through weakening the opponents. The only problem is that they are trying to do exactly the same thing to us. Thus, at least half of our energies must be spent defending ourselves and are unavailable for creative problem-solving. If both sides were not spending this energy on self-defense, think how much more attention could be focused on creating a solution that would honor *both* views!

When we look at the vast resources spent on weapons build-up worldwide, that is on ''defense,'' the wasted energy in this sort of situation is clear. Yet many of us would argue that you can't simply let down your defenses with someone you don't trust. It seems that the obvious question, in love and work as well as war, is, "How do opponents come to trust one another?" And it seems reasonable to assume that as we learn to build trust among "opponents" in our everyday lives we will each be contributing to the world's collective consciousness about how to safely disarm.

Principles are easy to articulate: if I trust you and open myself to your view, you will be more apt to feel open and supportive of my view. Putting such principles into practice is vastly more difficult: Who is going to take the first step toward softening and yielding? What if I do, and you betray me?

The solutions to this dilemma are to come to a deeper level of self-trust, to seek a wider perception and understanding of one another, to open our hearts without sacrificing our strength, to take a step outside and above our attachment to having things our way in order to see more of the whole picture.

As long as we continue to play power games, nobody will ever win. You cannot solve a problem at the level of the problem — in this case, at the power (third chakra) level of perception. As long as having one's own way is seen as more valuable than resolving conflicts so that everyone gains, we will continue to experience struggle. Only when one or both parties act from the broader perspective of compassion (fourth chakra), will we experience a shift in the rules of the game of life.

To act in the spirit of compassion is to place as much value on understanding you as I do on having you understand me. The larger picture which results is one that includes your perspective *and* mine in dynamic relationship to each other. The relationship that results from compassion is one in which both people feel recognized and empowered, so that they no longer feel the need to prove themselves by besting the other.

Compassion, the fourth chakra perception, is simply an updated version of the Golden Rule: I realize that whatever I do to another, I am doing to myself because I have deeply experienced how interconnected my life is with others' lives. I recognize that my respecting you is an act of self-respect, which in turn engenders your respect. The offer of recognition and respect can only come from one who has that feeling of self-respect.

Compassion is the foundation for resolving power struggles, not because of some arbitrary religious code, but because of its practicality. It is simply a perspective that sees more, respects both parties, and seeks harmony over victory.

## What's the Payoff?

So far, in considering the various approaches to resolving power struggles, I have tried to suggest that you have something to gain personally by developing your ability to get beyond the power struggle. In this section I'd like to summarize some of the personal fringe benefits you can expect to reap from developing yourself in this way.

As you learn to accept aspects of your humanity that you'd been unaware of — that is, as you stop projecting these qualities onto others — you find yourself feeling confident and assured in a much wider variety of situations. It is as if, by expanding your self-awareness, you have expanded the size of the world you can comfortably live in. You are at ease in situations that you used to avoid or fear. You have your full capabilities more readily available to you, which gives you a sense of having a wider range of options for handling any situation you encounter. You have a greater sense of self-reliance and adequacy. Like George Catton after he discovered his latent capacity for tenderness, you no longer need to depend so much on others to perform functions that you have not developed in yourself.

You also have the capacity to empathize with or understand a greater variety of types of people. As you come to accept and understand the variety of "sub-personalities" within yourself, you become open to other people as you have never been before. This empathy is felt by them and they like being in your presence. You are now able to enjoy and learn from people you once tended to avoid.

You may even find that you are *seeing into* others and *feeling with* others in ways that defy ordinary reason. The deeper you come to know all aspects of your own being, through taking back your projections onto others, the deeper is your capacity for understanding others. In short, as you become more empathic toward yourself, so you increase your empathy toward others.

If you are engaged in any line of work where dealing with people is essential, you will find your relationships becoming smoother and easier. You know what motivates different types of people. You don't treat everyone the same way. Yet you do treat everyone with empathy and respect, which makes them enjoy working around you. Being with you enhances others' self-esteem and well-being. As a result, they are more ready to listen to your advice, buy your product, or give you their trust.

Your life gets easier as you become more self-aware and self-accepting because you are now participating in the natural flow of human evolution. The direction of evolution has always been toward increasing complexity, that is, toward more harmonious cooperation of increasingly differentiated parts. As a living being becomes more differentiated, as it develops its formerly latent capacities, it tends to become more accepting of others, thereby fostering more harmonious cooperation.

This process of "live fully and let live" has cumulative effects. As more and more beings come into their appropriate relatedness with others, the world becomes a more highly evolved system. A sense of interdependent harmony can come to prevail over the sense of strife and alienation.

Following the direction of evolution, while it does require effort and attention, is much easier in the long run than trying to maintain the status quo. Development, expansion, and change seem to be givens in this life. "We must grow or die," say the biologists.

The evolutionary development that seems to be calling our species to attention in these times is the ability to focus energy in the heart, to feel love and compassion while maintaining our sense of power and individuality. The human species has the opportunity to learn how to have the best of both worlds — power and love — as we find that developing empathic understanding brings with it a new kind of power.

# thirteen: Guidelines for Communication

There are ways of communicating which tend to open up dialogue between people. There are other ways that tend to shut it down. In this chapter, you will find a catalogue of hints for opening dialogue that can be used in conjunction with your efforts to apply the principles offered in the previous chapter.

— *Express what you are thinking, feeling or wanting* now *in* this *relationship with* this *person.*

Do not bring in incidents from past relationships to bolster your position. The same thing holds true for past situations in this relationship. References to the past seem to confuse the issue at hand, often because your partner may feel that you are comparing or equating him to someone in your past, which is always a dangerous thing to do. If you look at the similarities between this and some past situation you fear will repeat itself, you'll bring an attitude of fear into your present interaction. Your mind becomes conditioned to expect the feared but familiar occurrence, rather than something completely new and unique. The habit-dominated part of the mind thrives on familiarity and avoids novelty. To grow into more satisfying ways of relating, you need to allow yourself to be pleasantly surprised.

I tend to violate this guideline quite often, usually with unfortunate consequences. As a relationship researcher, I tend to look for patterns of behavior which repeat themselves over time. In my relationships with men, for example, I've tended to mold my wants to theirs to insure greater harmony. If I share this insight with my partner, he may interpret my comment as a statement that he's just like all the other men in my life.

The reason that I want to share this insight has nothing to do with giving my partner the impression that he is one of many men in my life. In my eagerness to offer the insight, however, I sometimes forget my aim, and that is when I bring about confusion in the communication between us. My aim is to let him know that I am sometimes a person who will hide her feelings in order to keep the peace; and I would like his help in overcoming that tendency. In other words, I really wish to say, "Please understand that it is a risk for me to disagree with you, but I'll take the risk when necessary so that our relationship will be built on honesty, rather than pretending." To communicate this, I don't really need to bring up situations from the past. He'll listen more easily and get my message more clearly if I stick to talking about *us*, here and now.

— *Express your feelings in positive terms. Say what you're* for, *not what you're* against, *what you want, not what you don't want.*

It is much easier for another person to receive your message when it is stated positively, rather than negatively. It's less apt to set off a negative or defensive reaction. A clear and positive statement of what you want from the other makes it more likely he will act on it. And it opens your own mind to having things go well for you. It shows greater mental focus and commitment to use a phrase such as, "I want your attention,'' as compared with the more passive and negative phrase, ''Why don't you ever pay attention to me?'' The active, positive phrasing is easier to listen to because you are presenting yourself as more open, more vulnerable.

To simply complain or attack your partner requires much less emotional courage than to state your need positively and hopefully. This way, you are risking rejection and in effect saying to the other, ''I trust you enough to be vulnerable with you, to let you see my need and my softer side.'' Usually, when you let others see you more deeply, their regard for you grows.

*— In any emotionally-loaded interchange it works best to allow one person to express a viewpoint fully before the other offers an alternative or opposing view.*

In other words, don't interrupt the other while she is having her say! She won't be able to listen to you anyway. Once she has expressed herself fully and feels you've given her your attention, she'll be much more open to listening to you. If you find that she keeps interrupting you, even though you have listened attentively, ask her gently to hear you out. If this doesn't work, let her talk some more. Apparently, she has more to say before she can attend to you.

If you should find that you are with a person who just can't stand to hear any other viewpoint, you may need the help of a third-party consultant, such as a counselor or mediator. Video taping and replaying your conversations can be extremely useful in helping such a person realize what is happening. Videotaped feedback is often most effective because the person sees and hears her behavior with her own eyes and ears.

If you and your partner are both highly motivated to increase your ability to listen to each other during difficult, perhaps emotional times, try the ''Active Listening'' ritual discribed in Chapter Fourteen. I teach this technique to nearly all couples I counsel, and even the most psychologically sophisticated are amazed to find how useful such a simple practice can be. Active listening is simple, but it often takes a lot of practice and concentration to really be able to do it. I generally find I need to coach couples in my office for several hours before they can use this method effectively in conflict situations at home. So don't expect instant results.

    — *When expressing feelings you know will be upsetting to your partner, describe your several mixed feelings.*

Most of us feel at least two things as we struggle to communicate difficult feelings. We feel our own need or point of view, and we feel reluctant to hurt or displease the other person with what we are about to say. It is much easier for the other to listen to you when you show concern for him as well as yourself.

    This guideline only works when you truly feel empathy or concern for the other. If your expression is not genuine, that will show. For example, in the difficult matter of firing an employee: "I don't mean to upset you, but you're fired," just won't work. You need to show the genuine inner struggle that has occurred or is occuring between the differing viewpoints within yourself. If you can show that your position has been arrived at thoughtfully, you'll find that your message can be received more respectfully, and with less upset directed at you.

    — *When you want another to behave differently in relation to you or a common task, try using the phrase, "I want..." rather than, "You should..."*

Most people resist being told how they "should" behave. It feels like a put down or a judgement. You are setting yourself up as a judge of what is best for another person. Most of us are not wise enough to judge others, and it usually backfires when we try.

"I want you to put your tools away at the end of the day because I like a sense of order." This statement shows respect for the other. It tells her about you, not about her. You're no authority on her, and she knows it. She'll probably resist you if you try to be.

In Transactional Analysis terms, "You *should* always put away your tools," comes across as a Parental remark, which tends to evoke a Child-ish response: resentful or withdrawn acquiescence, rebellion, passive aggression. If you desire an Adult-to-Adult, or equal, transaction rather than a Parent-to-Child transaction, be careful not to put yourself above the other by the language you use.

**fourteen:** Rituals for Getting
Through the
Power Struggle

**The rituals** in this chapter are intended to assist
people who may be engaged in power struggles, but who feel
a commitment to learning from differences, rather than
winning at the other's expense. They may be self-guided, or
initiated and guided by a third party, depending on your
circumstances.

Most of the pair rituals can be done in a group setting as
well. Likewise, most of the group rituals can be modified for
use by two people.

## Pair Rituals

### Telling Your Stories

Sharing vignettes or chapters from your own personal life
history can be a heart-warming way to come to know and
understand someone. Two people who have told each other
about how it was for them growing up often find themselves
developing a deep feeling of rapport. This can help them to
overcome disagreements and misunderstandings that may
arise later.

Often it helps to tell your stories on several different occasions, focusing on a new aspect or chapter each time. For example, on one occasion, you might each in turn tell about your religious upbringing or the spiritual dimension of your life from childhood to the present. At another time you might share your history regarding the development of your sexuality and attitudes toward sex. Still another time could be devoted to your political consciousness, and so on.

There should be plenty of time allowed for this process. Some people do it on long plane or auto trips. Others prefer to have absolutely no distractions. It is important that when you are the listener, you offer your undivided attention to the other, so that you can really begin to feel how it might have been growing up with this other person's life experiences.

## Empty Chair Dialogue

This ritual will help you to take back feelings and qualities you may have projected onto another. You start by thinking of a person with whom you are having a fairly intense emotional conflict. This could be a friend, a parent, a co-worker, a child, a lover, or a spouse. Sit down in a chair and place an empty chair so that it faces you. Then imagine that this other person is sitting in the empty chair.

Begin the dialogue with the imaginary person opposite you. Speak out loud, just as if the other were actually present and able to hear you. Tell this person your feelings and wants with regard to the relationship. Or tell her what she does that you like and dislike. Talk about whatever comes into your mind. It doesn't need to be rational; and it doesn't need to be something you would actually say to the person in real life.

After you have begun the dialogue from your own chair, move to the empty chair and speak back to yourself as if you were the other person talking. Again, say whatever occurs to you in response to what has just been said from the other chair. Then switch chairs again and be yourself once again. Allow the dialogue to go on for a while, until you feel some change in the relationship between the two voices.

Finally, ask yourself how it felt being the person in the empty chair. Was it familiar or foreign, pleasant or distasteful, easy or difficult? Is there perhaps a chance that the person in the empty chair also represents a part of your personality? If it was easy to be the other, perhaps you are ready to acknowledge this aspect of yourself. If it was difficult, perhaps you are not ready to accept the part of yourself that is like this other person.

## Inner Dialogue in Writing
Instead of using two chairs to symbolize your conversation with another person — and the part of yourself that this other symbolizes — you can also carry on a dialogue in writing. This is like writing a play for two characters, with yourself as one. Be sure to allow the written dialogue to continue for several pages. Many people get discouraged or impatient and stop the process too soon. You may surprise yourself if you keep up the dialogue well beyond the point where you began to feel like stopping.

## The Safespace
The "safespace" is an actual physical location in the home or workplace that the two of you share. It is a place for you to enter together when you wish to re-establish or reinforce a tone of harmony and acceptance of differences.

You'll need to set aside a room, or part of a room (or outdoor spot), to be designated as your safespace. Decorate this place with ritual objects which for you symbolize qualities such as peace, calmness and reverence. Many people place a simple candle in the space which they light upon entering the room. Others place a small oriental carpet, possibly a prayer rug, on the floor where they then sit facing each other.

The safespace ritual calls for both of you to enter the space silently and sit together, facing one another or side by side, whichever position feels appropriate. Upon entering the space, adopt an attitude of "we-ness" — an attitude which focuses on the *interdependent relatedness* between you. Each of you surrenders your individual point of view and becomes receptive to a larger view which embraces both.

This is an entirely non-verbal, non-linear technique for resolving differences. Sometimes partners feel a new quality of energy passing between them as they sit for a few minutes in their safespace. Sometimes they intuit, or see, symbolic images of healing or harmony, which they may choose to talk about later, upon leaving the safespace.

The amount of time spent in the safespace may vary from five minutes to an hour. It is a good idea to agree beforehand on how much time you will spend there and to have a kitchen timer or gentle alarm clock to keep time for you.

The safespace ritual is a way of retraining your body and mind toward an attitude of openness or receptivity to another. To open yourself enough to sit silently with another greatly facilitates understanding, once you again begin to exchange words. It is as if simply placing two bodies in the same space, with no wish to control or change each other, accomplishes a subtle chemistry which draws attention to your commonalities, rather than your disagreements.

## Sentence Completion

This activity is designed to help couples and co-workers see the world from each other's viewpoint. Photocopy the list below and give a copy to each partner. Each of you may then complete the sentences with the first thing that comes to mind. Then exchange forms to see how the other has responded. Follow up by discussing the similarities and differences in your values, needs, backgrounds, and perceptions.

I wish

My mother never

My mother taught me

My father never

My father taught me

My brother(s)/sister(s) thought I was

My mother wanted me to be

My father wanted me to be

I struggle to

Every day

I'm afraid

In ten years

What I want most is

What I wonder about is

I never

In my family

My friends think I'm

My job

I respect people who

If only my partner would

If only my boss would

My favorite meal is

The best vacation I ever had was

When I'm alone I

I wish I were more

Someday I hope to

I don't want people to know about

I often feel

I almost never feel

People in a hurry

People at work

I've always wanted

I hate

## Do It Yourself "Marriage Encounter"

The formal Marriage Encounter process consists of a weekend spent in a retreat setting where couples are encouraged to communicate about things they may not usually talk about. They are each given a set of questions and asked to: (1) reflect on each question alone; (2) write their responses to each question; (3) sit together and read their responses to one another; and (4) discuss any feelings or reactions they have to each other's responses.

It is a very simple, straightforward workshop format and one which couples (and other pair relationships), could easily duplicate on their own. (This is not to deny the values of the support of a group, an understanding facilitator, and a "retreat" environment.)

The questions below are designed to be used by couples and co-workers at home or work during an uninterrupted block of time. Set aside at least four hours for the entire process, two hours alone time and two hours for sharing and discussion.

1. In what ways do you wish your partner were more like you?
2. In what ways do you wish you were more like your partner?
3. If your relationship is to (get through this impasse or) grow to its fullest, what do you think you need to learn to help this to happen?
4. What do you think your partner needs to learn?
5. How do you think your partner sees your current situation (the current status of your relationship)?
6. How do you think your partner would answer question 5?

## Resentments and Regards

This ritual, also known as R & R, is a way to clear the relationship of stored-up or withheld feelings. It is meant to be done about once a month as a sort of relationship tune-up.

Partners agree in advance to set aside an hour for their monthly R & R. The ritual goes like this:

1. One partner shares *resentments* (things the other partner has done or not done that have brought on negative emotions) for about ten minutes, while the other simply listens;
2. The first partner shares *regards* (things that have engendered positive emotions) for another ten minutes, while the other listens;
3. The listener comments or asks questions (but does not explain or defend him/herself) for about ten minutes;
4. These same three steps are carried out by the second partner.

The objective of this activity is the *exchange* of feelings and information — not the resolution of conflicts. Couples and co-workers often need to learn to "sit" with their differences without necessarily having to *do* anything about them. It is important in this ritual to understand that our emotional states are constantly going up and down (what we call "positive" and "negative" emotions), and that it is quite important simply to be *aware* of events which seem to trigger such up and down movement.

## Do You Mean?

This activity offers a way of checking perceptions about any possible hidden meanings in what the other is saying. It is also an opportunity to reality-test catastrophic (or overly positive) expectations and assumptions.

A time is set aside to talk together about an area of some disagreement or difficulty between you. Person A starts the conversation with a statement of his/her feeling or position. (*e.g.*, "I'd like to go out alone tonight.") Person B responds with one or more queries that begin with "Do you mean...?" (*e.g.*, "Do you mean you're trying to get away from me?") Person A says only "yes" or "no" to these queries. As long as A's answer is "no," Person B continues with more "Do you mean?" questions until he or she finally gets a "yes" answer. (*e.g.*, "Do you mean you'd like to go somewhere where you can be quietly by yourself?"..."Yes.")

Following A's statement and B's queries, B then initiates another round, starting with a statement of B's wants, intentions, fears, opinions.

This exercise offers partners a chance to exchange information about what is going on beneath the surface appearances in the relationship. The questions probably contain even more information than do the statements; people tell a great deal about themselves by the questions they ask.

## Sharing Withholds in Reverse

This ritual is similar to the R & R process in that it affords a chance for the periodic clearing of relationship conflicts. It also places a value on empathy, listening for what the other is feeling in addition to expressing one's own feelings.

Partners mentally scan over their interactions during the past week. Then A takes five to ten minutes to tell B what A imagines or intuits that B might have felt but did not express (withheld) this week. B simply listens and does not confirm, reject, or explain. After A is finished, B says, "Thank you," and takes a turn sharing intuitions about what A might have withheld during this same period.

The emphasis in this ritual is on *hearing* each other's hypotheses with an open, non-judgmental, experimental attitude. Once both have had a turn, then it is time to confirm or correct each other's perceptions.

## Common Vision

Sometimes when two people are in a power struggle, they are fighting not about *where* they wish to go together but rather *how* to get there. For example, a husband and wife may agree that they want more fun in their lives, but her proposed solution might be for him to take a more relaxing job, while his may be that he work harder so he can retire in five years.

In this activity, partners seek to reconnect with the overarching or superordinate value that brought (or brings) them together. Satisfying the customers, serving humanity, improving the quality of life, spreading love and good feelings, learning how the world works, creating a happy home, developing the capacity for unconditional love — all these may be seen as examples of superordinate goals in love or work.

The process for arriving at a succinct statement of one's goal is as follows for each person:

Start by answering the question, "What do you want from life?" Then, ask "Why? — Where will that lead?" attempting to broaden (rather than narrow) your focus to include more of the context of your life (other people, your organizations, your loved ones, etc.). Write down this answer. Then, ask again, "Why? — Where will that lead?" allowing the context of your response to broaden even farther. After both people have done this several times, compare your responses to find what values are common or shared. Once people see the overlap or commonality in their goals, the way is paved for more cooperation.

If it occurs that the two parties involved have *entirely* divergent values, it may be time for a parting of the ways, and successful accomplishment of this could provide a temporary common goal.

## Communication Cycles

It is often impossible to determine who "started" a power struggle. Harry and Rochelle, for example, share a *communications cycle* common to many couples: the more Harry withdraws into his own private thoughts, the more Rochelle nags to try to get his attention. And the more Rochelle nags, the more Harry withdraws. Who started it? It is impossible to say for sure.

We might diagram Harry and Rochelle's communication cycle like this:

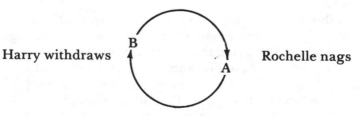

If we see the interaction as starting at point A, then Rochelle started it. If we see point B as the original action, then we could say Harry's withdrawal set the cycle in motion. Obviously, it takes only one to start such a cycle. But it takes two to keep it going. Either one could interrupt the pattern at any time and thereby bring about an end to it.

Communication cycles such as this become habitual in

long-term couple or work relationships. A common pattern in the work context: the more supervisor Fred oversees employee Tom's work, the less Tom seeks Fred out for feedback. And, of course, the less Tom seeks Fred's opinions and feedback, the more directive and supervisory Fred becomes.

Any long-term relationship will tend to bring out the polar opposite tendencies in two people. This can lead to increased competitiveness or enhanced complementarity. In order to promote cooperation, it is often helpful for couples and co-workers to sit down together and reflect on the pattern(s) or cycle(s) in their relationship and on whether these are hindering their communication.

If you wish to do this, begin by looking over the examples listed below. These are some of the communication cycles I have found to be most common:

He rationalizes  She criticizes

He becomes bolder, more risk-taking (e.g. with money)  She becomes more cautious (worries about how little money they have)

He demands                                    She withholds

He becomes lethargic,                         She becomes
passive (lets circum-                         domineering, takes
stances control him)                          charge

He becomes                                    She becomes cold
insulting (when
angry)

He hides,                                     She interrogates,
is evasive                                    is suspicious

Of course, *he* and *she* can be interchanged in all these examples. And any of them can apply to love or work relationships between people of either sex.

Using this last as a stimulus for your discussion, now try to pinpoint one such cycle in your relationship. Think of a few instances when this pattern was operating. Then take turns telling each other how you felt during these situations. Try to help the other sense what it felt like to be *you* at that time. While your partner is speaking, do not interrupt. Give your complete attention and try to feel what is being said.

After you have both expressed your views and feelings, see if you can think of one thing that each of you can do or say to interrupt the cycle the next time it occurs. Do not expect miracles, but continue to apply your "antidote" whenever you notice yourselves in the habitual pattern. When the other successfully applies the antidote, show your appreciation.

## King/Queen For A Day

Sometimes couples get into a rut where one or both feel as if they are constantly compromising or accommodating to the other. This can even occur to two people simultaneously. Each feels that, "Obviously *I* always give in and let my partner have his (or her) way."

A good way to illuminate such a situation is to choose one day on which he will be king, and another day on which she will be queen. On your day — and try to make it a non-work day — you both do things that *you* want to do, either together or individually. The other willingly goes along with your directives, sincerely trying to help you enjoy your day to the fullest. This is an especially good exercise for couples in the midst of a power struggle because it gives an experience of agreement and common purpose for a change.

To discover the relationship rut you are in as a couple, answer the following fill-in questions, first individually and then together, comparing and then modifying, where appropriate, your individual answers:

Whenever he (she)

I tend to feel

What I tell myself is

and what I usually end up doing is

Her (his) reaction to this is often

This makes me feel

Then what I do is

We often find ourselves in this kind of cycle, in which, whenever I

he (she)

What I'd like to be able to do when she (he)

is

What prevents me from doing this is

In order to help us change this pattern, what I need to learn is

What he (or she) needs to learn is

## Identifying Your Personal Pattern In Relationships

To discover your own individual relationship pattern, begin by filling in the following blanks:

1. I tend to be attracted to men/women who are (name as many qualities as you wish):

2. Because of their (one or more of the above qualities)

they tend to treat me (or react to me)

This makes me feel

3. I tend to attract men/women who are

What I appreciate about such men/women is their


What I dislike is their

4. The things men/women really like about me are

5. The things I'm usually criticized for are


6. When my partner and I aren't getting along, my reaction is to

This often "causes" my partner to

7. In relationships with men/women, I'm usually the one who

My partner generally responds to this with/by

8. I wish I could be more
in relationships.

Then
wouldn't keep happening to me, and I would be able to

Now that you've answered these questions, reflect on how your answers illuminate the recurring themes in your relationships. Do you tend to behave similarly in all relationships, or does your behavior change depending upon the person you're with? What other consistencies and inconsistencies do you see? Is your style of relating satisfying or unsatisfying to you? Can you imagine what a more satisfying style would look and feel like? What is it that prevents you from behaving this way? What would you need to learn in order for your relationships to be more satisfying?

## Group Rituals

### Advice for the Other

This ritual illustrates how common it is for people to give advice to (or make judgments about) others that reflects things they themselves are also needing to hear.

In this group activity, each person is given a 3 x 5 card and asked to write on it the name of one person in the group to whom they'd like to give some strong advice. They are then asked to write their advice on the card. Next, each one is given the chance to read his/her advice aloud to the group, this time substituting their own names instead of the other's. For example, "Tom (Sam's boss), you need to learn how to listen" becomes, "Sam, you need to learn how to listen."

This ritual, when shared by a group (such as a work team) becomes an excellent vehicle for illustrating how relationships (even at work) can be a path to self-awareness, since we so often notice in others the very things we ourselves need to learn more about.

### Round Table Role Exchange

This activity is useful when two or more sub-groups, or representatives from these groups, are in conflict. Perhaps the groups are attempting to negotiate an agreement, or perhaps simply trying to understand one another's view.

The ritual involves asking each "side" to imagine themselves to be on the other side(s) and then to write down: (1) their overall purpose, aim, or reason for existing; (2) what they have to have (at a minimum) in order to achieve their purpose; (3) what they would ideally like to have to achieve their purposes with more ease; (4) how the other side(s) could assist in the pursuit of their aims.

Then, a mock negotiation process begins, where representatives from one group "act as if" they are representing (one of) the other side(s).

When the game is over, participants discuss what they learned about themselves and the other during the process. The things groups most often learn in this activity is that the other side(s) have very similar overarching (superordinate) goals. The conflict is generally around how to allocate resources so that all can contribute their part to the achievement of the goals. When groups recognize their interdependence — that they actually need each other — the way is paved for mutual creative problem-solving, rather than bargaining and power tactics.

## Fishbowl

This is a very popular activity for two groups seeking better understanding of one another. Each group agrees to allow the other group to observe it in action. In a work setting, we might have a meeting between the secretaries in a certain office and the managers. First, the secretaries sit in a circle and discuss "how it feels to be one of us" or other shared concerns. In another circle, around the outside of their circle, the managers sit and quietly observe. After a time (15-30 minutes usually) the managers go into the center circle — the "fishbowl" — and allow the secretaries to observe their discussion of the same topic. After this second round has been completed, the two groups join again as one group and discuss their feelings and observations.

## Confronting Differences

This activity is designed to encourage confrontation of controversial matters and to reduce fear and avoidance of conflict. A facilitator asks participants to:

1. In a preliminary period of silent preparation, look at each member of the group and try to identify your main area of disagreement with, or criticism of, him.

2. Invite, as your partner, someone with whom you think you may have an important difference, on a matter about which you feel strongly, but have never openly explored with him. If he agrees to work with you, the two of you should invite someone, not already paired, to be your monitor. Thus the whole group will be divided into triads, each consisting of two opponents and a monitor.

3. Begin the triad session by trying to define the issues of possible conflict. Don't pussyfoot. At the beginning, it is better to exaggerate than to minimize the antagonism. Be blunt, forthright, outspoken! The monitor should intervene if she thinks either participant is going soft or smoothing over the real difference.

4. When both opponents agree on a definition of the controversy and some of the specific ways in which it has appeared, let each in turn try to trace some of the *personal history* which led to his present outlook, feelings and behavior. This may be a soliloquy which begins with early memories and reviews significant persons and incidents which played some part in forming attitudes.

5. When both have given their account of the genesis of their positions in the controversy, each should try to state the view and feelings of the other. The test is: can you state your opponent's position clearly and fairly so that he will respond, "That's it exactly. You understand me!" The monitor may help, if needed, but should feel comfortable remaining silent.

6. When each has been able to state his opponent's position to the satisfaction of that person, review what has now happened to the feelings of each about the issue and about the other person.

7. Rejoin the group. Each monitor will report for her triad on the definition of the issue and some of the historic determinants which emerged. Then each of the opponents will repeat to the whole group the gist of his antagonist's position, trying to make it as clear and acceptable as possible.

8. After each triad has finished its report, the group as a whole should address itself to the question of what the exercise has accomplished. Do any members see themselves or one another differently now? Would it be worthwhile to try this technique again, later, in connection with other controversies?*

## Image Exchange

This activity is designed to be used with groups or individuals who are actively engaged in a controversy. It was described by Ronald Lippit at an informal talk at the National Training Laboratories' Higher Education Lab, Bethel, Maine, 1969. Two groups, the "Blues" and the "Greens," were known to be at odds on several points. A consultant (Dr. Lippit), who was brought in to help resolve the conflict, started by meeting with each group separately. In his first session with the Blues, he asked them to talk about their areas of agreement with one another, their assumptions about how the Greens felt about these issues, their feelings about the Greens, and their assumptions about how the Greens felt toward them. He asked if he could tape record this discussion and explained that eventually each group would have the opportunity to hear the other group's tape.

After each group had had its first session, a second session was arranged, during which each group again met separately with the consultant, this time to hear and react to the tape recording of the other group's first session.

---

*(adapted with permission from *Expanding Your Teaching Potential,* Susan Campbell, New York: Irvington Publishers, copyright 1983.)

The third session was a joint one, involving the consultant and both groups. By this time, each group had had a chance to air its views and feel supported for them, to check out its assumptions about the other group and to be heard and at least partially understood by the other group. At this point many of the false assumptions and stereotypes had already been clarified and only the areas of real conflict remained to be dealt with.

Last year, as a consultant for a new experimental college, I modified Dr. Lippit's design for use in a three-hour "conflict resolution workshop" for students and faculty of the college. The controversy centered around ratification of the college's proposed constitution. My intervention occured in the following stages. First, I asked participants to group themselves into three sub-groups: those who favored ratification of the constitution; those who did not favor it; and those who were undecided. I asked each group to spend half an hour getting to know each individual's reasons for being in that particular group (thereby building a feeling of support and understanding).

I then asked each group to briefly share with the total group the essentials of their separate discussions. The three sub-groups then reconvened, to try to agree on their goals for the college, and how they thought their positions on the constitution supported the attainment of these goals.

During this time, the sub-groups were confronted with the *values* implicit in their stances, and with whether their values really supported their goals.

Much re-thinking and re-evaluation occurred during this session, and since it was done among people who all shared the same point of view, there was little tendency toward polarization or defensiveness.

Next, each group was asked to share publicly its goals for the college. As it turned out, the three sets of goals were nearly identical. Thus, we had identified our first major area of overlap or agreement.

Then, each group selected a spokesperson to speak with the spokespersons of the other two groups regarding the various plans for reaching these common goals. This was to be done in a "fishbowl" structure, with all participants sharing. An atmosphere of collaboration had already been established, since we were all working toward the same goals. Where serious conflict did arise, the spokesperson for the "undecided" group was in a unique position to act as a mediator, since he was by definition aware of both sides of the conflict. He provided a model for the others for containing the conflict, rather than externalizing it or projecting it outward, showing the futility of polarizing the problem.

As the three spokespersons talked together, from time to time we would take a break, allowing each spokesperson to reconvene with his group in order to take a reading on where the group stood in relation to the others. As communication blocks were identified between spokespersons, the groups lent support and feedback to their spokespersons, aimed at resolving communication barriers.

After two and a half hours, the "undecided" had all taken a side, and over half of those who had been for or against the constitution had moved into the undecided group. A new compromise was not reached until a later meeting, but people did truly communicate with and have an impact on one another. They changed from resistant to open postures, and they learned that conflict resolution is more productive and realistic if the feelings of the opposition can be understood and entertained along with one's own.*

## Active Listening

The purpose of this exercise is to give individuals and groups an experience that shows them how well they hear and understand the conversations in which they participate. This is an attempt to illustrate how difficult accurate communication can be.

---

*(adapted with permission from *Expanding Your Teaching Potential*, Susan Campbell, New York: Irvington Publishers, copyright 1983.)

Group members form pairs and are asked to discuss a position that they have taken on some issue. The issue may be anything from how the participants feel about U.S. foreign policy to the pros and cons of open marriage. One person is the talker, the other is the listener. There is only one basic rule which must be followed: The discussion may not proceed unless the listener can repeat back to the talker what the talker has said, in a way which is acceptable to the latter. After fifteen minutes, the participants switch roles. A variation on this exercise is to have a third person sit in and function as an observer, giving feedback to the participants on what is happening.

People are frequently shocked to discover how little they understand of what the other has said. Remember, the purpose of this exercise is to understand the other's position, or to explain your own position. It is not designed to convince someone else of the rightness of a certain point of view. It also becomes clear that arguing is usually much easier (but less effective) than simply trying to understand or to be understood. Some discussion questions you may want to use after the exercise are:

1. Was it easy or difficult for you to repeat back what your partner said? What was difficult about it? What made this difficult?

2. Did you concentrate on your partner's idea, or did you find yourself thinking of your own point of view?

3. Did you and your partner agree or disagree at the end of the exercise?

4. What have you learned about talking to someone else?

5. What have you learned about listening to someone else?

# ⊗ fifteen: Beyond the Power Struggle

**Power struggles** come in many forms. They can be protracted or temporary, destructive or light-hearted, pervasive or circumscribed. And they can be resolved by changing your actions or changing your thinking. In this final chapter, I will review the hows, whys and whens of power struggles in a concise and easy-to-remember summary.

*— Close loving or working relationships can help you expand your consciousness and broaden your perspective.*
Over time you learn to include another's perspective alongside your own. This gives you the capacity to deal comfortably with a broader range of situations, to empathize with and understand more different types of people, and to adapt more easily to changes in your environment.

*— Expanding your perspective to include other viewpoints does not mean abandoning your own position.*
You come to see other realities in addition to your own, not instead of it. Such expansion does, however, often bring you to a new relationship with your original view. For example, you may come to feel less attached to your original

way of seeing or being, while at the same time maintaining and honoring your own unique view.

— *Each of us sees the world through the filter of our own wants, preferences, values, and past experiences.*

Differences in point of view are perfectly natural. Yet any one person's view represents only one angle or perspective on ''the truth.'' Attachment to your own viewpoint as the only way or the best way is the primary cause of power struggles.

— *Most peoples' attachments are based on fear: fear that we won't be respected, fear that we won't get what we want, fear that the other is against us in some way.*

Because of certain either-or assumptions we have learned, we act as if only one person in a conflict situation can be satisfied; that if one wins, the other must lose; that if one is right, the other is wrong. These assumptions lead us to treat others as if they were against us much of the time, and to armor ourselves accordingly. Prepared for a fight, we often get what we expect.

— *Some power struggles are necessary and useful, especially during the trust-testing stage of a relationship.*

Many are an unnecessary waste of energy. If you wish to eliminate the unnecessary struggles from your life, you will need to learn a new way of thinking about your relationship to others, a way that assumes it is possible for both you and the other to get your needs met — to be ''right.'' Such *both-and* thinking helps you to relax your rigid hold on being right or getting what you want. It makes you easier to listen to and to respect.

Such relaxation does not mean that you give up asserting yourself. It simply alters the attitude from which you assert yourself. You see the other's viewpoint more clearly and can respond more appropriately to it, with concurrence or with any objections you may have. Instead of a fear-based, ''I have to have my way'' attitude, you assert your position in a more relaxed way, a way that communicates confidence and self-respect. This increases the likelihood that others will respect you. When your way of being communicates openness and respect, you draw to you openness and respect from others.

— *The harder you try to maintain control, the less in control you usually feel.*

Everyone needs some sense of control in life. Yet it seems that the only way to attain a deep and abiding sense of being in control is to surrender to what life offers you, to give up your rigid hold on having things turn out a certain way.

Likewise, the only way to attain a sense of real security is to surrender to the insecurity or uncertainty of your existence.

When you adopt a Security/Control attitude, you are attempting to gain your sense of security through controlling youself and those around you; for example, through seeking to have others regard you in a certain way. This means that you are not open to, and therefore not able to perceive, other ways in which they might regard you. Thus, by adopting the Security/Control attitude, you tend to shrink the size of the world you can comfortably live in.

— *In close love and work relationships, where interdependence is essential, all attempts at controlling the other eventually backfire.*

To foster satisfaction in such relationships, aim your communication toward understanding and being understood, not toward trying to control, impress or otherwise get the person to do or think as you wish.

— *If we can find peace in our own hearts, we are in some small way helping to heal the dis-ease of our world.*

The war and competitiveness that we see in the world around us mirrors our inability to find peace and harmony within ourselves and in our personal relationships.

— *Moving beyond power struggles, and the either-or thinking that engenders them, requires a transformation in consciousness.*

We must shift from Security/Control thinking to Growth/Discovery or Unity/Participation thinking. There is evidence that our culture may now be undergoing such a shift, a shift that could spread to the entire species. This transformation may be necessary for humanity's continued survival.

— *While conflicts seem to be caused by differing needs or ways of doing things, the real cause is in the meanings people attribute to these differences.*

In intimate relationships, for example, rarely do two people have exactly the same need for contact at all times. But it is one's interpretation of this fact that leads to suffering or acceptance. If, for example, the difference is interpreted to mean "she doesn't want to be close right now...therefore she doesn't love me," struggle may ensue. If, however, you recognize that there are many reasons why another may need time alone, then you can more easily accept momentary differences in needs. If differences are not automatically seen as threats to the relationship, you will be able to talk about them and come to understand them more easily.

Co-workers very rarely have exactly the same way of doing a job. But again, what meaning do you give to this difference? Do you feel your ability is being questioned if your boss asks why you did a job the way you did? Do you perhaps feel your boss is trying to control you? Can you question your boss and allow your boss to question you without implying a threat to either person's competence? If you can, then your differences will lead to mutual learning instead of discomfort.

— *Many intimate fights are unconscious ways of adjusting the distance between partners.*

People fight when they want more closeness. They fight when they want more distance. But usually our fights seem to be about something other than these simple needs. People tend to avoid acknowledging a deeply felt need if they fear their partners may be unresponsive to this need. Instead, they will often pick a fight about something less directly linked to their most basic needs. This seems safer somehow. If couples could more easily accept their differing needs, they would be able to communicate more honestly.

— *It's not what happens to you that makes you happy or unhappy with your life, but how you handle what happens to you.*
If you handle things in a way you can respect, then you will accept life. If you handle your life's events in a way that makes you feel inadequate or contemptible, then you will resent life, or those around you, for putting you in such a predicament.

— *Whatever you resist in life keeps coming back to you, demanding your attention.*
If you always try to get your own way, in order to avoid feeling dissatisfaction, you will often be dissatisfied; if you always need people to love you, you will find yourself feeling unloved; if you constantly seek order in your life, you will be plagued by chaos. Life keeps confronting us with those events and experiences that we have not learned to deal with. In relationships, our partners and co-workers often appear to be at the source of our frustrations when they are more likely just mirroring back to us those aspects of reality with which we have not yet found a satisfactory way to cope.

— *The power struggles between people reflect the power struggles within people.*
We don't get emotionally involved in a power struggle unless we are also in a state of inner conflict.

— *When another person's behavior or attitude evokes a negative emotional reaction in you, there is some aspect of yourself of which you are unaware or unaccepting.*

If you are able to establish an open dialogue with this part in another person, this clears the way for a new and more accepting relationship to yourself. Through dialogue with another, you expand the boundaries of your sense of self.

— *Many couples are attracted to one another because each partner has qualities the other admires, and perhaps secretly wishes to have.*

All of us deny certain qualities in ourselves, and many of us seek to regain the lost traits by joining with a partner who exhibits them. With continued contact, we may come to learn these qualities from each other. When this occurs, there is no longer cause for struggle.

— *An interpersonal relationship is a living system with interdependent parts functioning to some degree as a unit.*

A change in one part of the system sends changes reverberating through the entire system. For example, if you become more sensitive to your partner's feelings, your partner may in turn become less hypersensitive, that is, less bothered by your "insensitivity." If you stop nagging, perhaps she will stop withdrawing. In a living system, one person's change does not occur in a vacuum. It is always felt and responded to in some way by the other person. If you want your partner to change, change yourself.

— *If you wish another to treat you in a certain manner, try treating that person in this same manner.*

Love engenders love. Openness engenders openness. Fear and suspicion engender fear and suspicion. Many people simply need permission to express the higher aspects of their natures. They need to feel it is safe to do so. Thus, somebody has to make the first move.

— *Each one of us is responsible for the quality of our own inner state, no matter what happens to us in the external world.*

No one is to blame if you are experiencing anger and frustration, not even yourself. However, you do have some choice in how you respond to whatever conditions you find around you. Our first-impulse, knee-jerk reactions to things that bother us are not the only responses available.

— *At any moment, in a potential conflict situation, you have the choice either to de-fuse or escalate the conflict.*

If you wish to de-fuse a potential struggle, to "turn the heat down," don't become aggressive or defensive. These are the most common reactions to feeling hurt, frustrated or misunderstood. Instead, try to hear what the other is saying and feeling and then, once the other feels heard and is thus able to listen, express your own viewpoint. Remember that your wish is to be felt, heard and understood, not to overpower, convince or prove yourself right. In addition to de-fusing the struggle, this approach is more likely to win you lasting power and influence with this other person.

— *Positive expectations about another's motives or intentions engender positive outcomes.*

For example, if you expect that the other sincerely wants to hear and understand you, you will communicate in a tone that is more open (less offensive or defensive), and thus easier for the other to hear.

— *To expand your range of choices, experiment with non-habitual ways of dealing with your negative emotional reactions.*

When someone does something that provokes an instantaneous negative reaction in you, it is as if they have pushed a button on a machine, and that machine has reacted automatically. In order to become more fully human (conscious) and less machine-like (unconscious), it helps to intentionally behave in ways that are not your habitual or automatic (sometimes seen as your "natural") ways.

— *Power struggles are resolved more easily when
participants follow basic communication guidelines:*
> • Express what you are thinking, feeling or wanting
now in this relationship with this person. Do not bring in past
incidents from this or other relationships to bolster your
position.

> • Express yourself in positive terms. Tell the other
what you want, not what you don't want; what you're for, not
what you're against. It is much easier for another to receive
your communication without defensiveness when it is phrased
positively.

> • Don't interrupt. Allow the other to express his
position fully and to feel understood, before you offer your
view. Once he's expressed himself fully and feels you've
given him your attention, he'll be much more open to
listening to you.

> • When seeking something from the other, the
phrase, ''I want...'' is received more easily than, ''You
should...'' Most people resist being told how they ''should''
behave.

— *If you are caught in a cycle of blame and
counter-blame, attack and counter-attack, it may be time to
look for the softer, more tender feelings which lie beneath the
surface.*

Most harder or sharper feelings cover over deeper,
softer, less easy-to-articulate feelings, such as a longing to be
closer, a need for reassurance, fear of being hurt, and so on.
When partners are able to recognize and express the feelings
underneath the feelings they are struggling over, the power
struggle may dissolve right then and there.

— *Resolving differences in sexual appetite and rhythm
can be a means of attaining inner balance and overcoming
self-centeredness.*

To achieve harmony, compromise is necessary. If your
partner does not enjoy sex, you will not enjoy it fully either.

This motivates you to pay attention to *both* the other's needs and your own, bringing an expanded quality of consciousness to your actions.

— *The types of relationships you attract to you can be seen as mirrors of your level of inner harmony or self-awareness.*
When you develop a more harmonious relationship between your inner polarities and "opposites," you will find yourself attracting more harmonious relationships with others.

— *The personal payoffs for learning to resolve power struggles are:*
• You feel confident and assured in a wider variety of life situations as you rediscover more and more of your personal potential.
• You have the capacity to understand and empathize with more different types of people.
• You may come to develop a deep almost telepathic rapport with some people, thus giving you more complete insight into what it means to be a human being.
• People will enjoy being in your presence because you treat them with respect. Being with you enhances others' self-esteem. As a result, they are more ready to listen to your advice, buy your product, give you their respect.
• If people come to believe and act as if other people are friends rather than adversaries, we are likely to see more relationships where resources are shared rather than hoarded. When this occurs, more resources actually become available to more people. The world starts to feel like a friendlier place and we become less fearful.


Learning to live without unnecessary struggle is a lifelong process. For most of us, it will require shedding old thinking habits and choosing to value *seeing* and *understanding* over *winning* and *being right*. At times during this process, it may feel as if you are losing power, as others ignore your views at the same time that you are open to theirs.

If this happens, don't despair. The rewards of both-and thinking are different from the rewards of either-or thinking. As you change your priorities from *being right* to *understanding and acting on all relevant information*, your very definition of what it means to be powerful will change. As you find room in your heart and mind for seemingly contradictory ideas and feelings to peacefully co-exist, you greatly increase the appropriateness and long-range effectiveness of your actions.

# ⊞ epilogue

## On Nuclear Disarmament

The threat of nuclear disaster may be the most terrifying collective pain the human race has ever experienced. But in spite of the horrors involved, the fact that it is a *collective*, world-wide experience may stimulate the awakening of human consciousness that is needed in these times. The radical change in the behavior of nations that would be necessary for world peace requires a radical shift in human consciousness as well; a shift in values, a change in perspective.

Right now we seem caught between our instinct to survive as an entire species and the wish by certain political subgroups to maintain their sense of power and control by dominating other political subgroups. On the one hand we identify ourselves as part of the body of humanity with a strong instinct for species survival and evolution. On the other hand, we identify ourselves as Americans or Soviets, Israelis or Arabs, Moslems or Christians, with a wish to see our particular way of life spread throughout the world. A more subtle political subdivision is of course the division between the world's haves and have-nots, or between the superpowers and peoples of the third and fourth worlds. The arms race as currently run can also be seen as a conspiracy by the haves to keep the have-nots in their places.

Selfishness, greed and lust for power are not the only forces behind our current situation, however. There is also the knotty problem of face-saving. According to the rules and norms of international relations, it seems that to reduce one's armaments significantly is viewed as an act of weakness.

While most of us can see the absurdity in the way nations attempt to bully and impress, we fail to notice the parallels between the relationships of nations and the relationships of ordinary people. Ordinary people can play a role in the shift in consciousness. We would not be at war as nation-states if we were not in conflict within and among ourselves.

If we could truly allow two or more conflicting impulses within our psyches to peacefully co-exist, that would be a beginning. Most of us were taught that one is either strong or weak, selfish or generous, happy or sad, But if you look carefully at youself, you will probably see several seemingly contradictory impulses all seeking recognition or expression in your personality. When you can see and accept the full cast of characters in your inner drama, you have taken a major step toward peace of mind.

Such acceptance, of course, represents a radical shift in perspective. You can include more in your total field of vision than you once could. This will lead to a shift in your relationships with others, to accepting people who disagree with you, and to seeing the world from their perspective as well as your own. All this requires that you make room in your consciousness for things to co-exist that you once thought were incompatible.

Perhaps you have had the experience of loving and hating someone at the same time; this gives you a glimmer of what I'm talking about. Either-or thinking makes us narrow-minded, unable to see the "big picture" needed for understanding the complex problems of our world. We need to learn to think in ways which embrace paradox, in ways which allow us to love a person while hating what she does, or to feel both fearful and courageous, both hopeful and despairing at the same time.

Dr. Robert Fuller, well known peace activist and former president of Oberlin College, asserts that world peace is unlikely until humanity can devise what he calls ''a better game than war.'' Peace, according to Fuller, is a non-event, an absence of something, rather than a goal-directed activity, or game which can excite people's interest. Perhaps we humans need to discover the excitement and challenge of expanding our personal power and intelligence through coming to think in both-and terms.

If we can stop identifying ourselves as disconnected from others and our inner impulses as contradictory to one another, it follows that we would see ourselves as human beings first and only secondarily as members of national, political, or religious groups. This shift in consciousness can start in our everyday lives — in our families, marriages, friendships, and workplaces. If we can begin at home to see differences between people as several facets of a whole, rather than as contradictory viewpoints competing for validity, there will be plenty of room on earth for the peaceful co-existence of *both* Americans *and* Soviets, *both* Arabs *and* Israelis, *both* Moslems *and* Christians.

It is a challenge that requires the efforts of everyone on the planet. If this challenge can ignite the interest of a large enough and diverse enough segment of the earth's people, perhaps we will succeed in creating a better game than war.

# MORE BOOKS WITH *IMPACT*

*We think you will find these Impact Publishers titles of interest:*

**ACCEPTING EACH OTHER:** *Individuality and*
*Intimacy in Your Loving Relationship*
*Michael L. Emmons, Ph.D. and*
*Robert E. Alberti, Ph.D.*
*Softcover: $9.95     1991     240pp*
Enrich your loving partnership by developing six key
dimensions: attraction, communication, commitment,
enjoyment, purpose, trust.

*NO-FAULT LIVING*
   *Gerald Albert, Ed.D., with Scott Michel*
   *Softcover: $8.95     1991     144 pp*
How to stop blaming yourself and everyone else in
marriage, child-rearing, love, friendship, business.

*LIFE CHANGES:*
   *Growing Through Personal Transitions*
   *Sabina A. Spencer, M.S. and John D. Adams, Ph.D.*
   *Softcover: $8.95     1990     208pp*
Seven-stage guide to successful handling of major
changes: relocation, job upheaval, divorce.

*YOUR PERFECT RIGHT:*
   *A Guide to Assertive Living* (Sixth Edition)
   *Robert E. Alberti, Ph.D. and*
   *Michael L. Emmons, Ph.D.*
   *Softcover $8.95   Hardcover $12.95   1990   256pp*
The assertiveness book most recommended by
psychologists. Nearly a million in print. Step-by-step
procedures, examples.

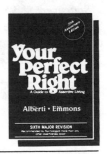

*Since 1970*
*The Foremost Publisher of*
*Self-Help by Qualified Professionals*

*Please see the following page for more books.*